Ways God Speaks
Through His Word

TRESSA OLDEN

Library of Congress Control Number: 2021947371
ISBN: 979-8-89465-033-3 (sc)
ISBN: 979-8-89465-034-0 (e)

Printed in the United States of America.

Integrity Publishing
39343 Harbor Hills Blvd Lady Lake,
FL 32159

www.integrity-publishing.com

CONTENTS

FOREWORD

The goal of this book is to uplift, share His goodness, and bring hope in all areas of our walk with Jesus.

You'll be surprised, although I may not know you personally, we've gone or are going through some of the same trials and valleys.

Coming through we can see how God had His hands on us. How He carried us over to the other side. I have learned along my journey to apply the WORD. It must be lived and lived out loud as doing, not lip service.

It is important as a child of God to give attention to the Word. The more time we spend in the Word, we are able to see the goodness of our Savior. the more of His goodness we see brings us trust, and in trusting God we are blessed.

My prayer is that you'll be inspired, and changed, knowing that God is the same today, tomorrow and forever.

Tressa Olden

Keep Writing

Once God has placed within your heart
A dream, a desire, a vision
You must within yourself realize
Through God it will come to fruition

God places on the heart of man
To encourage just write it down
The things that will surely be a blessing to others
That would cause that old devil to frown

The devil does not want us to be free
In bondage is where he wants to keep us
So, we will live defeated lives
That render our worth the cheapest

But God surely knows just what He wants
BE VICTORIVOS in Him do not fight it
IF God has laid it on your heart
My child sit down and write it.

Written by: Tressa Ann Olden

He knows

I sat down to interview, a woman whose life she states was not proper or prim

As we sat across from each other, she immediately said, buckle up, what you're about to hear is grim.

She admits she wasn't rocked quietly to sleep like other babies

She didn't have a mother's loving arms holding her

She can't remember her reading a bedtime story or her soft voice and guiding hand molding her

Uncertainty was a call that followed her, a tender mother's care, her soul certainly lacked.

Someone to talk too, to share with and buy pretty dresses

The crystal vase of her life had a crack.

Though as she grew self-control she did not have. Rebellious, self-willed and very bitter

Why she thought was I not like other little girls, she felt nothing good in life was going to fit her.

With her security gone, she continued her same ways

On her own in a world all alone

She didn't realize even in her confused place

God was watching her every move from His throne

"I am who or what you need me to be, I can love you through the pain

Come close, open up your heart to me, you're my child there is so much to gain.

Now she looks contently over her life. Remembering when she submitted saying yes

And allowing the Savior to restore her whole

And set her sights on heavenly things despite life's quest.

Written by: Tressa Ann Olden

Covid 19

911 the day, the earth stood still for many
Grief stricken were those and lost lives were plenty
BUT COVID
Has made its way
Into our lives every single day
We must pray!

It's a silent killer and moving rapid
With your own two hands you may unknowingly tap it
We've gotta pray!

We really don't know when or where it comes from
So, we are sheltering in place and staying at home
People are dying by the thousands, businesses are closed, so many jobs being lost
Airplanes are grounded, medical supplies are limited
My God Are we counting the cost? Pray
Schools, are desperately trying to reach our children, locked in with no way out
Teachers feeling helpless, churches are empty, the silence of it all makes one shout
PRAY!

Arena's closed, no sports, no gym, many of our parks shut down
And day to day more closers are added, my God, I feel I might drown
Pray for me pray!

My God is a daily cry for me, this flesh, I'm in has had it
Each day I wake up to the news, something new to the list is added.
Pray!

Yes, we wake up many mornings, taking this world we live in for granted
but as each day unfolds, we view the news and our hospitals are now in a panic
pray children pray!

And yes, hospitals are few, for the needs we are facing
Presidential staff, and Heads of state, constantly updating, constantly pacing
We're in and pandemic, deaths recorded all over the globe
We are instructed to be still, many working from home, and some just wearing a robe
WHILE THERE, PRAY!
God is waiting for our fervent cry,
There are so many lives just waiting to die
Saints of God pray!

We who are God's must pray to change
Fasting and praying will rearrange
Hands in the air, and knees to the ground
I know will turn this situation around
They say it's gonna get worst, before it gets better
I'm counting on Jesus for I know He is greater
If we Just pray!

Written by: Tressa Olden   2020

Riches

He does provide daily all things, anyone could only hope for
Peace, love and understanding, He overflows them more and more
He certainly supplies every need, according to His riches in glory
His promises are true, He stands on them
Take time and thank Him for your story

Written by: Tressa Olden   2008

I Believe

I believe that Jesus went to the cross unblemished just for me
I believe he suffered helplessly to set the sinner free
I believe he forgives all our sins and loves us through the fault
And God's only son shed his blood and through it I was bought

Written by: Tressa Ann Olden

He!

Sometimes in my room I feel lonely
When I feel this world as let me down
I'm glad the One who controls it all
Gives smiles that erase a frown.

He lifts me in the noonday
or even late at night
He is the source of all my joy
My soul in Him delights.

I can go to him for everything
He listens attentively
He always gives me good advice
I don't always agree

He is so ever patient with me
I know there's much to learn
My soul cries out for understanding
In him my heart does yearn

And even though I don't always agree
I know what He says is right
This flesh that embodies our very being
With choices it tries to fight

But I'm learning each day to heed his advice
For He loves me and wants what is right
He has taken my soul from the depths Of Hell
And lead me to His Marvelous light

Written By: Tressa Ann Olden

Let's

Let's just be real about what is going on
Let's not hide what is really inside
Let's come to grips with all the pain
And put away the anger, the pride
Let's strive to forgive and rebuke in love
Each and every one we meet
Let's learn to love and care for one another
For its Satan we must defeat
Let's walk in the light that others might see
Our good and glorify God
Let us walk in love, given Mercy and Grace
And our feet with peace be shod

Tressa A. Olden

Rare Jewel

Remember well and bear in mind, that a virtuous woman is hard to find.

And according to the bible being a wise woman I'm told

The stature of this woman is worth her weight in gold

Like a pearl she is soft deep within her heart, daily going to God to remove blemished layers

Seeking Him always for knowledge and wisdom, remembering Him always with prayers

Her strive is make other's as she is, in love patience and understanding

Like the pearl that is formed from the inside of the shell, she knows it is God inside doing the commanding

Quick thinker, innovative, always moving, pressing ever so gently toward the mark

Her light it shines so brightly, with rainbow colors it reflects through the dark

She is a priceless, precious gem, a rare jewel standing out in a crowd

She doesn't allow problems to isolate her, her faith speaks out very loud

A valued gem she is highly sought after by many a brother one hears

That matching set that makes her most expensive, though to find her it may take him years

Knowing her wisdom comes from God, she continues on through the shadows of night

Like a rare pearl her heart is set aside from others and it absorbs and reflects her plight

So, honor her highly, esteem her greatly for she is a most precious stone

A chosen vessel, a gift from God, standing firmly on His promises alone

Written by: Tressa Olden   2008

Renewed

Lost with no direction, clueless of things to come

Someone shared Jesus with me, as we sat alone in my room

I had so many concerns, racing over and over in my mind

I still did have a clear direction, not a glimpse or hint of any kind

I was shared that God's grace is sufficient, but for me I had trouble seeing

After all, am I worthy to ask and seek, to change from this person, I'm being?

Will Jesus forgive my sin? I asked the person in front of me praying

If you ask Him with a sincere heart, He will do it without delaying

What if I fall again, will He still be there when I need Him?

His word says He will never leave us alone, He died for all men's freedom

What if I make a mistake, in my trying to do all that's right?

God knows your heart. He understands and will guide you to the light

Thank you for sharing this blessing with me, my life I want renewed

You have given me hope in troubled times and a future bright and viewed

Tressa Olden   2008

What's Important

We purchase our brand-new dresses
We shop for new shoes too
Our hat purse and stockings
We're blessed! Half of what's in our closet new

As Christians we must remember
While on this Christian way
Clothes are not important
As how we act what we do and what we say

I've learned that being a Christian
Does mean a lot to us
But certainly not having new fashions
And causing all kind of fuss

But coming out and learning about the savior
Our purpose and surely our roles
Now that ladies, is more important
That all our designer clothes

(Paraphrased from a six-year-old memory)

Recited by: Tressa Olden

Friends

Why is it hard to find a friend?
I mean a really true one
One that you can tell things to
And feel that they are genuine

I don't mean a friend who is with you
Until you're not together
I mean a friend who sticks by you
In any kind of weather

Not one who only likes
When you have something to give
But one who cares and shares the load
And helps with troubles lived

I'm glad that I know Jesus
He truly is my friend
I can tell Him my most inner thoughts
Over and over again

He says he'd never leave me
And he has kept to His word
For when others have turned their backs on me
HIS SWEET SOFT VOICE I'VE HEARD

So, let not your heart be troubled
He will be right by your side
Ask Him anything you want or need
And your feelings, please don't hide

Just believe He will never leave you
Don't be ashamed to drop that pride
He came to earth to be an example
Trust Him He will be your guide

So, head high just keep on going
Jesus is a true friend who will go all the way
He's a friend I can depend on Him
Each and every day!

Tressa Ann Olden   2005

Knowledge/Life

God knows just how much we can endure
He never gives us more than we can bear
Though daily we must go to him
And all of our burdens share

Be honest, sincere and fervent!
Share exactly with Him what you need
He's there to hear your every desire
Trust him he will take heed

He knows the deepest parts of us
Our spoken and unspoken request
And loves us through the faults we have
And for us wants only what's best

And so. we must go to him daily
If you can go down on your knees
For the God of this universe takes care of us
Father, Son and Holy Spirit agrees

Written By: Tressa Ann Olden

Basketball

I love the game of basketball it teaches you to compete
Its play on a court for forty-eight minutes
Against an opponent you try to defeat

They say to really be good at this game you must play it with heart
Assemble your team chose your ground after the jump ball
The game you must start

It's run defend throughout the game with teammates who think like you do
You work collectively as one unit
One mind leaving the opponents without a clue

The object of the game is to defend and score, until the final minute
The team who scores the highest points
They're the ones who will surely win it

And real life like the game of basketball you find you will compete
It's played until your life is ended
And Satan is whom you'll meet

They say to really be good at this race you must instill in your heart
The word of God and daily prayer
And his love you must impart

It's pray and keep praying all through the day with believers who think like you do; study
your bible and love one another
Daily go to him and renew

The purpose of the race is to go to the finish, keep striving and never give in
The one who endures when Jesus returns?
A crown he will surely win

Written by: Tressa Ann Olden

Because of love

God's son JESUS died for me
Because of love He went to Calvary
Because of love many witnessed His blood
being shed
Because of love they put a throned crown on His head
Because of love he carried a wooded cross
Because of love His mother felt sorrow, felt loss
Because of love He paid the ultimate price
Because of love He is the perfect sacrifice
Because of love He died to set me free
Mankind can now have eternity
Because of love

Tressa Ann Olden   2004

16

I'm Healed

I see myself whole for that's how He sees me
I believe my healing is imminent
I'm trusting His touch will quiet the doubt
What Jesus can do is not limited
I pray to Him daily believing that I will receive
The strength that my body sorely needs
I go to Him daily and give Him my all
My spirit within me agrees
I need Him to touch my body and mind
And control it to benefit Him
I lift Him up and praise His name
No doubting outcome of grim
Laying here on my pillow He brings peace to my mind
And in Him is where I find rest
Content He knows just what I need, for daily He answers request

Written by: Tressa Olden

Healing

Someone said the way to heal is simply to forgive.
The way to move pass all the hurt is let go and simply live

Forgiving means letting go of all the anger and pain
Keep moving toward a better you there is so much more to gain

God forgives us as we forgive those, he awaits to mend our heart
He says my child I'm here for you, now you must do your part

Reach out to me I'll set you free you can in me abide
I love you just the way you are without that selfless pride

Let me make you from the inside out, and make all enemies behave
I heard the prayer you prayed to me and fervent sincerity you gave

Now go in peace the battles not yours, just continue to follow my lead
And when you feel offended again, forgive, for you have been freed.

Written by: Tressa A. Olden

Does God Know?

Does God know what a teen goes through? Does he know the daily temptations of what not
to do?

Does he know the peer pressure they face in their schools? The teacher
counselor's oh so many rules

Whether to apply themself get good grades and excel, or saying no to
drugs so that we don't fail

Trying to abstain when all their friends say yes; standing up for what
They believe thinking above the rest

Does God know they're going to the mall, buying things they don't
need? When they should stay after school in order to succeed.

Does He know sometimes when their driving in their car?
Piling in without seatbelts they're not going very far

Does He care that being part of a group requires a name on their shoe?
Or the trouble they face when missing their curfew.

What is so wrong when mom and dad go out of town
Inviting friends over just to hang around

Well as a teen if God could just help them with one of these things
Before a serious relationship, before diamond rings

If God will allow them mistakes as they learn
To ease the questions, the thoughts, the concern
Then with God they should try the best they know how
Not waiting for tomorrow, they should be starting right now

With God and a parent, they will obtain the knowledge
For success in their life and going to college

God surely understands the life of a teen
And those informative years the questions in between

Growing up daily from childhood to adult
With God leading the way we'll get a great result

This will make mom and dad so proud
And assurance they want get lost in the crowd.

Written by Tressa A Olden   2003

Africa

A team was sent to minister in a foreign land.
They boarded a plane, said their goodbyes with bibles in their hand.

They faithfully took the assignment that God had placed before
He stood knocking at the door of their hearts
Each willing opened the door

The journey that was in front of them, not one of them could see
But trusting in the God we serve went forth victoriously

This team went out from our fellowship
and took the people God's word
Caused silence to become rejoicing from the Good News
that was heard

I know the people in Africa will never be the same
For the God given team who heeded the call
Unleashed the power in JESUS name

Mission well done

Tressa Ann Olden   2004

The lap of Jesus

Like a child I climbed up on Jesus' lap
To share my disappointments and concern
My failures and my heartaches
He responded my child there is much to learn

I told him about my mistakes and all the times
I had asked for forgiveness
He responded my child if you ask, I forgive
Not tomorrow right now with the swiftness

I continued to share all that was in me
The tears began to flow down my face
He comforted my fears and dried all my tears
And shared His merited favor of Grace

So, I sat for a while talking to my Jesus
There was so much that I wanted to say.
He listened ever so attentively before
Instructing sending me on my way

After time I got down from His lap
But I left everything in his hand
He responded my child now go in peace
For it is all in my command

I looked in his face as he told me those words
So great were the things I had brought
He responded my child the price was paid
With My shed blood, your life I have bought

My heart does rejoice from my Saviors embrace
Him loving me enough to stand in the gap
So daily I have learned to go to him
And climb upon His lap

Written by: Tressa Ann Olden

Christmas

Despite what consumers might say Christmas is not in July

July, we celebrate Independence Day and watch the fireworks fly

July is the time for vacation across country or over the seas

It's the time when family's gather together and picnic under the trees

A tree is not being decorated; the holly is not yet in bloom

The mistletoe isn't hung over the door to kiss the one entering the room.

Though Christmas is definitely coming it brings with it the season of cold.

We bundle ourselves in coats and scarfs for it pierces the inner soul.
Its candy canes and lollipops, Its garland with glitter and glow.
Its eggnog and reindeer and Santa's ho, ho, ho.

God designed seasons in the beginning from summer we have
six months to buy
But I DECLARE to you early shoppers, that Christmas is not in July.

Written By: Tressa A Olden   2003

Under God

Under God contentious words
The most controversial I've ever heard
Our very existence is found in these
To remove them are totally absurd

Nadeau argued before the court of Supremes
These words are an unlawful means
that one's equal rights are violated by
the saying in the Pledge so it seems

Long before it was Mike, you, and me
There was no visible life land or sea
The earth and its fullness all belonged to God
He spoke with power "Let there be"

God spoke into nothing and made something
God breathe the very existence of life into man
And the big bang theory heard all over the world
Is a mystery most fail to understand

My God controls these United States
The world and they therein
He now sits in the heavens with Jesus His son
But Under God is where it began.

Written By; Tressa Ann Olden   2004

A quiet place

A quiet place
A place of peace
All come together
And never cease

He meets us there in this quiet time,
And fills our hearts, with pure sunshine

Joy unspeakable, love over flowing, resting in
Him and always knowing

He cares for us in our quiet place,
He meets us there in our quiet place,
He speaks to us in our quiet time
Just me and Jesus

Written by: Tressa Olden   2019

Purpose

I got up early this morning, and I began to pray,
I wanted the lord to guide me, throughout this
entire day;
so, I got down on my knees, and I began to moan,
It wasn't very long before my answer was shown

"A purpose driven life", a book in which I read
It made me stop and ponder, the directions in which to head

The verses will transform your thinking,
in what God as made you for,
The reading is exciting and revealing
it keeps you wanting more.........

So, join us and yes be praying for all the unique small groups
who will meet on a weekly basis no need to jump through hoops,

No need to be a scholar. Rick Warren will handle that task
No need to be a born leader, if you can't do it all you have to do is ask?
One will surely be provided, a home and vcr is all you need,
If God is speaking to you this day, all you have to do is heed.

For he is handing out blessing, forever name on the list
He says; where two are three gathers, agreeing, He would surely be in the midst
The bible says, with two fish and five loaves of bread
With Jesus handing out the portions, five thousand hungry people were fed

So, all Christians keep reading, keep fasting, keep praying
and see what forty days with Jesus will do!!!!
He's standing with his arms wide open, this day he beckons to you

join us won't you

Written by: Tressa A. Olden   2003

Glow

An illuminating spiritual light flowing upward Behold the figure of angels motioning the power of a sovereign God who hears

Written by: Tressa A. Olden

A letter to Jesus

I've come too far to turn around
Though at this moment I'm feeling bound
By the pressures of life

One giant step forward and countless steps back
I'm seeking your face Lord my life is off track

You have never given me more than I could bear
Please Lord at this time I need you there
weighting pressures of life

I'm seeking you now though at peace in your word
You are helping me stand through your promises I've heard

You have taken me through storms for you are the Captain of my life
You fill me with your Spirit and steered me from strife
But the pressures of life.

Are now weighting me down
The smile that you gave me
My mirror shows a frown

Lord I need your strength you took to the cross
My need feels so desperate my need feels like loss

I'm lifting my head I'm pressing everyday
You said you'd be with every step of the way

I'm standing still listening needing to hear your voice
I'm lifting you Lord I'm making that choice
Through the pressures of life

Written by: Tressa A. Olden

Cleansing

The rain is God's purification of all the earth's debris
It's a cleaning process that only God's understands
that bring life to every blade of grass and tree.

Each drop individually is so tiny; standing
alone hardly visible at all; but when thousands
and thousands keep pouring from heaven in places
it resembles a wall.

Water coming from heaven, water refreshing the day
Like the Spirit the Son left here with us; when he
descended for our sins he did pay.

The Spirit is purification it stands with the Father
and Son. It leads us and guides us through many a
storm and will keep us until our day is done.

Like the rain controlled only by God! It's quick
but covers the mass. The Spirit it quickens and
cuts both ways; given by him if only you'd ask.

Written By: Tressa A. Olden

31

Compelled

As I walked into the sanctuary, it now seems long ago.
A bible clutched into my hand; of things I've come to know.

As the door was opened, many faces to see, some smiles some somber looks
Didn't shake one hand, but could clearly see, like me there were many with books.

As I entered so quietly and took a sit, a prayer I could hear in my ear
of thanks going up and blessing coming down and a Savior who's ever so near

I sat there still longer, and read silently of a peace that has no understanding
Of a God who still cares, a love that abides, and a Friend who is very commanding

I continued to sit, I wanted to know. the reason I had come to this place
This was not in my plan, not on this day, the spirit spoke gently "Its Grace"

A tear I did shed, it's now in His hand, I have turned it over to Him.
As the choir sang a song, it all came to me; all things in this life are not grim

Lift Him up they continued to sing, everyone in this place did agree
As I quickly joined in, something moved inside, something very familiar to me

I know this Man He died for me; He's the Savior of the world
I was taught early on in Sunday school for every boy and girl

This was all I needed, I was so overjoyed, what a day this had turned out to be
As I took my sit, the spirit spoke again, now this will set you free.

The words that went forth, was clear as a bell. All these people he spoke only to me
Of a God who still cares, and understands a wayward sinner's plea.

He gave us today, with yesterday's facts from the book he held tightly in his hand
The plan he laid out; a map would unfold of a Friend who was so in command.

Ask Him; just ask Him anything that you will. He will give you the help that you need
Don't leave here; don't leave the same way you came, the man in the front did concede

He said He came not to condemn the man, but came that he might be free.
He took the pain and bore the cross all the way to Calvary

Some came that day, and took his hand, not wanting their souls to be loss
For he spoke again, convicting words, we all must bear our cross

I left that day, knowing for myself that a work had begun in me.
All week I prayed and ask the Lord for the answer of unity.

This day I came and took his hand the choir was not what I heard
This man of God spoke once again, and compelled me with the Word.

Written by: Tressa A. Olden   2000

How

It's amazing a tree knows how to grow
Not only up and down but to and fro

And trees with needles referred to as pines
Are wide at the bottom moving up it declines

The mighty Oak with branches that extend
Timeless beauty with stories that never end

Maple trees runs up and down the street
Waving its broad leaves to everyone they meet

So many trees not everyone the same
Many varieties traits and names

Trees in autumn bring colors to the sky
Of reds oranges and yellows
captured by a painter's eye

They all have branches, trunks and bark
Many can be seen in an area park

The giant Sequoias got their start
With leaves and roots playing their part

A tree knows just what to do, it knows its season to change
It's intelligent enough by trait to know the size of growth and range.

It's just amazing this wonderful plant with a single main stem to the ground
As we look up, we ask ourselves, how far does the roots go down?

This is something that remains a puzzle I guess a mystery for now
As we consider this perennial plant we enjoy, but it leaves us asking how?

Written by: Tressa A. Olden

Don't Give Up

When I felt life was not worth living
I was bitter I was angry and tired of giving
He never gave up on me

This hopeless state I found myself in
No one to talk to no one to call friend
He never left me alone

He comforted me with His words from the Book
Written down deep in my heart
He controlled all the fears
He dried all the tears
And gave each day a new start
But He never gave up on me.

Each day I am trusting and praying to Him
He gives me assurance
My life though still dims
But He never leaves me by myself.

I know He will keep me
Through all this pain
I know through endurance
There is much to gain
Because Jesus never gives up on me!

Written By: Tressa A. Olden

Forgotten

Jesus has not forgotten you are not alone
He took grief, sadness and helplessness with him to his father's throne

He says I will never leave you. You chose to leave my side
I stand knocking waiting your return for in me you can abide.

The world can sometimes be very cruel unfriendly and downright cold.
But his love reaches deep in the soul of man and melts and icy mold.

His reach extends to you Hs child, His grace will never run out
It's like the oil the widow had free flowing an endless spout

In him you will find peace of mind love, joy and a new beginning
One who will stand right by your side on his team you are always winning

Give him a try, ok another try, this time stand fast don't move
Let him supply the things you need hold on and let him reprove

Just remember you must stand fast, you may waiver and sometimes fail
But get right up and start again don't stay down and become useless and frail.

Now lift him up and praise his name a true friend you have found
You will never ever be alone again for God is always around

Written by: Tressa A. Olden   2004

Jesus

Jesus Christ Savior at his birth
Visiting wise men knew what he was
worth; He came bled and died for the sins
of this world; to redeem all mankind
on this earth.

Written by: Tressa Ann Olden

Forty days

The forty-day campaign has come to an end sentiment echoed
"let's do it again

People were rejoicing and telling their stories of pain and failure
their successes their glories

Many look forward to hearing each week on what the pastor spoke
about and would only give a peek

Each Sunday he'd teach and openly share and one of the purposes
would surely be there

Ministry, fellowship, worship was taught Jesus's love and what he
bought

He shared with us the price that was paid the blood that was shed
the sacrifice made

In our small groups there was love overflowing Hearts being mended
and relationships growing

He continued to teach on Evangelism too, reaching the lost not just
in the pew

Discipleship a coming together, helping each other, making one better

With every purpose covered a celebration would come, to thank the savior
on where he brought us from

There is still much to know about why I am here. What drives my thoughts
what brings a tear

But God made us all unique not the same This powerful God knows us all by
name. He has given us the tools and the choices from strife. So, we can live

THE PURPOSE DRIVEN LIFE.

God's Love   Written by; Tressa Olden   2003

Homework

Homework, homework what a chore
Quiet time what a bore
"Get it done" mama shouts
concentrate figure it out

"Were you listening, did you hear"?
"What she told you was it clear"?

Write it down, then you will have it
Questions later you compare it

That was easy! got it done
Getting a clue makes homework fun

Written by: Tressa A. Olden

Grandchildren

Grandchildren are wonderful little persons; It's a parent and grandparents' joy
Whether God blesses you with sugar and spice are puppy dog tails for a boy
You love them through all of their questions with answers they will soon forget
But every time you see their smiles you'll answer again /no regret

They are very inquisitive in nature they are treasures grandparents adore

They are God's sense of humor of a gentler time you swear they have been here before
They are precious gems waiting to be polished; our dowry right down here on this earth
They are daily reminders of a sovereign God No ransom for what they are worth
It's the hugs they give you so willingly; It's the innocent way that they sigh
It's the way they say, "I love you grand" Oh my how times does fly

They are duplicates of your children repeated the antics and little things they did
It brings back memories of the younger years when they were still just a kid

We spoil them by buying them everything: Some needed and some just because
Then send them off with their parents and let them correct the flaws
So, these little people are diamonds; They are as valuable as gold in a crown They are the love
that was sent from heaven above. The place for which we are bound

Written by: Tressa A. Olden   2004 Inspired by: a grand

41

The Choir

Hallelujah, Hallelujah glory to GOD was shouted very loud
Praises dancing joyous singing spread throughout the crowd.
Enter into his gates magnify the most high
Hands held high in the air, silence breaks a cry
Jesus, Jesus someone shouted, a wonder to behold
Jesus, savior of the world magnificence untold
That's' the day the lord came in
That's the way the lord came in
That's just how the Lord appeared the day the choir sang

Written by: Tressa A. Olden   2003

Sovereign

He spoke about a savior, who hung upon a cross, He said he came
to redeem us back, for without him we would be loss

I listened ever so careful to gleam a message of hope. To share with
those less fortunate, and those who could not cope.

His message moved around somewhat, but one thing came out clear,
Sovereign, top the list and he spoke without conviction or fear.

He's sovereign my savior, He's sovereign yes indeed, he's blameless and he's faultless 'Once
bound and now I'm free.'

He paid the price, no excuses he paid it for you and me, He paid it without murmuring that
day on Calvary.

His smile lit up the room, as he continued to share the word. There is no one else like him
Again sovereign is what I heard.

He's sovereign, my savior he's sovereign, yes indeed he faultless and his blameless once bound
and now I'm free.

And as he closed his message. His presented case was made. He let us in on Elisha, a man
who became afraid.

But closing arguments suggest in life there are many turns, God is the one who is in control of
all the lessons learned, and he's sovereign my savior, he's sovereign, yes indeed

He's faultless and blameless once bound and now I'm free.

Written by: Tressa A. Olden   2003

If

If there were dreams the mind could conceive
If there were goals you had to stretch…. to achieve
If with faith you would only believe
Then God would work miracles!

Written by: Tressa A. Olden   2004

Intrigue

Intrigue a word that comes to mind as he sat across the way
This man so quiet his demeanor reserved for one we'd meet some day

Soft spoken was he at first we'd meet, A GENTLEMEN PLAIN TO SEE
God's hand had reached beyond the known and touched so graciously

It was no surprise my husband and I, had made a friend for life
God's plan, God's hand, was on this man, who seemed so filled with strife

I was taught as a child not to judge and old book though it's cover may be tattered and torn,
it's the sole of a man that's important to a God though life sometimes leaves us forlorn

God shapes us, and moles us, and gives us, the gifts with the natural eye there's despair, But
God, being God, and only he knows, they are his gentle angels unaware

As I sat in deep thought, God gave this to me, with his hand he allowed me to pen, about
this selfless man, his somber plight, and the man with the boyish grin

God loves us all in so many ways some ways we don't understand, But He' let's us know
with unspoken words (He's a treasure he's truly a friend

God bless you

Written by: Tressa Ann Olden   2003

Just like Daddy

Just like my dad he cared for me: from birth and through infancy

He fed me on milk, when meat I could not chew, and gave me
everything I needed, as time went on, I grew

When starting out to walk, I was up and sometimes down
But just like dear old dad, he was always around.

Instruction and knowledge things to help me learn,
Wisdom and understanding, oh how my soul does yearn.

Just like my dad he taught me how to pray,
Says you will need this child, each and every day

Continuing to study to keep myself strong,
Striving to do things right, and never do things wrong.

Unconditionally he loves me, just like my dad, which helps
me through rough times when life treats me bad.

He says I'll be with you, no matter where you roam;
No matter where you go you can always come back home

I walk so ever close to him, still needing much to grow,
Just like my dad did with me so many years ago.

I will follow in his footsteps, everywhere he leads;
He gives me the desires of my heart, and takes care of my needs

He shows me that he loves me, he has opened many doors
He says my child deny yourself this day the choice is yours.

I will never forsake you are leave you by yourself,
Daily read and study your bible don't keep it on the shelf.

When some nights are sleepless worrying to stress
Jesus cradles me in his arms and allows my soul to rest.

My child if you need me, for anything at all
Please do not hesitate just give me a call

And just like my dad did oh so long ago
Says my child I'm always near, and gives me room to grow

Written by: Tressa A. Olden   2003
Jesus /eternity

No respect

When I was just a little child, I heard this said in church
I didn't know the meaning then are even if it had worth

They would stand before the congregation and I could
clearly hear.
No respect for persons rested time and time again in my ear

When I grew up it still lingered there the question of what
it meant
The God I served the One I loved and surely the Son He sent

Could not have meant He didn't care for anyone at all
This surely couldn't mean the Savior did not hear our call

Grown I soon came to realize I was listening with still
child's ears.
The ones God gave me so long ago, when then I was only
5 years.

So, I took out my bible and began to search "no respect"
Just what could this be.
Whatever it meant I needed to know, because now it was
weighing on me.

The Bible clearly reads about a lot of things, many things are
yet to understand.
But reading and searching the scriptures each day, better
helps us define His plan.

He does not esteem one more than the other,
He loves us all just the same
If we're using the one talent, He gifted to us
Are many with fortune and fame.

He knows the purpose for which we are here
He knows the abilities we own
He knows the level and skills we can reach
And surely, He knows our groan.

So instead of no respect for persons that I heard
those years ago.
No respect of persons is what I now came to know.

He loves us all and cares for us, and can use us
Just as he will
Open to Him a willing heart and He does enhance the skill.

So, don't let society make you feel least. God doesn't
He uses what we've got,
Whether standing in front of the congregation or
Minister of the coffee pot.

Tressa A. Olden   2004

Original Design

Gods' designs are original, unique and one of a kind
There is no one that's exactly the same, no not one you will find

Question raised "what of a twin? You can't tell them apart
Outside to us they look the same, but God's looks on the heart.

I met a family, and their two children, certainly resembled one another
I'm sure that's true, we are made in His image, but looks are only to utter.

We're all so different He made us that way, our purpose to glorify Him
And when our differences come together, it's like flower petals to the stem

And though uniquely different they complete each other, the flowers they
know when to bloom.
As we let our lives avail to Him, we are like the butterfly from the cocoon

Written By: Tressa Olden

Passion

God touched the heart of Mel,
and gave him a story to tell.
Not one that has not been told before;
but one everybody should yell!

He took it all for me;
He went to Calvary
and Pilot washed his hands for he knew,
Though accused He was not guilty.

Crucify him they said;
"But I will rise again from the dead",
They mocked Him and beat Him all the way up the hill,
and placed a Thorne crown on His head.

Not a word against them did He speak;
Though in flesh our Savior grew weak,
He hung there so humble and bled for our sins
Giving His heritance to the meek.

Many torturing Him did not have a clue;
That a life in Him they could renew.
So, they pierced Him and nailed Him
to an old rugged cross;
"Father forgive them for they know not what
they do".

Rest assured on that third day He rose.
Appeared to His disciples, the story goes
He stood there and showed them is nailed
scarred hands.
resurrected from the death He had chose

Written by: Tressa Ann Olden

Performance

God began speaking to my heart as I watched the two perform
It was as if the spirit spoke out loud and set off an alarm

All eyes on these they continued to move so boldly without
saying a word
While throughout the crowd and around the room Gods praises
Could clearly be heard.

Their performance was flawless their motionless flow each
surely ordered by him
Their gift they shared received you're blessed time invested
Was more than a whim.

God spoke they listened still in silence they posed
Their presence a message for all.

God's gift to them sent love to many
As they mimed to answer His call.

Written By: Tressa A. Olden   January 2004

It's a personal thing (Serving God)

You cannot serve two-master's you will cling to one the other will want.

The bible is very specific; live life full there is no need to taunt.

Life brings us so many decisions what's right for us and oh what is wrong

The bible says deny yourself daily keep your mind set on the Heavenly throne

Remove far from me vanity and lies give me neither poverty nor riches

Feed me with food convenient for me and steer me from the devil's hitches

Accuse not a servant unto his master lest he curse you, and you be found guilty

Leave all the judging to God alone sin born we were all found filthy

There's a generation that cursed their father and doth not bless their mother.

We all must stand before the judgment seat of Christ. Why do you judge your brother?

There's a generation that is pure in their own eyes yet not washed from their own filthiness

Jesus came and died that we might live; to rid us all of the guiltiness

There's a generation whose teeth are as swords and their jaw teeth are as knives to devour.

We will all have to answer when Jesus returns but no one knows the day or the hour.

Why look at the moat in thy brother's eye and considered not the beam in thine own

Jesus' blood was shed for all mankind not just the righteous alone.

Give not that which is Holy to the dogs neither cast ye your pearls before swine

my foot have I held his steps I have kept lest they trample and my soul decline.

So, I say in this life get to know him things we do don't all have to agree

The choice you make in your personal walk, surely does not have to suit me.

Our Savior and Lord gave us life, from each strand of hair he knows all

For when the Master pricked your heart only you could answer the call.

I wasn't in on your conversation I don't know what Jesus told you

The bible states clearly to love one another and that's what I strive daily to do.
So, let's love right through agreeing to disagree let Jesus Christ only to judge

Be patient therefore brethren until the coming Of the Lord; against one another don't grudge.
As we worship and fellowship together Let us live and let live God's correction.

Till we all come before him on the Great Judgment Day to enter His Heavenly perfection.

New Year's Resolution 2003   Written by: Tressa A. Olden

Ask

It's not ok when confusion consumes you
It's not ok when others you mistreat
It's not ok when you choose what persons to love
Being selective with those whom you meet

When God is nothing but love
He says to love everybody
Don't be confused open up he will teach you how

It's not ok
Ask God, Ask now!

Written by: Tressa Ann Olden

I love you

I love you in spite of what others may say
I love you because Jesus first loved me
He looked beyond all faults we have
AND LOVES UNCONDITONALLY

Written By: Tressa Ann Olden

57

Cherish me!

Our vows say to love and honor
It goes on to include obey
It says what God has join together
Let no man put away

Our vows talked of our commitment to one another
Precisely in sickness and health
It went on to say as we stood there together
About the riches and wealth.

A golden band that encircled our fingers
That represents our endless love
A never-ending symbol we share with each other
Sanctioned by the Lord above

A vow before God not taken lightly
Committed to over years won't perish
With love and sincerity, we exchanged our hearts
With God's blessings we will always cherish

Written by: Tressa Ann Olden

Concerned

God is concerned with the sinner, as well as the poor man in need
He makes himself available to all of us, each circumstance and situation he'll not impede

To the rich He says give up all and follow me; the poor widow He explained she gave more;
Many, stand around scratching their head from His teaching; puzzled by the love for sinners
He does out pour

Give to those who to you are less fortunate; love your enemy as you love yourself
In that great day when our Savior RETURNS to this earth;
Go with him my child, don't be the one left.

Obey His word, go to the hi-ways and tell your story, no one knows it quite like you do
Share His Love and His mercy from your walk and from your talk

A road frequently traveled by few

Written by: Tressa Ann Olden

Stand

Where do I go from here Lord?
My pillow I have wet with my tears
Which way do I turn for some relief?
In you there is no fears

I pray continually as my bible informs
I love those who shun my name
I reach out to those less fortunate than I
I try loving everyone the same

Though from day to day I'm having a struggle
This flesh seems to think it can win
I have learned not to lean on my own understanding
And keep trying over and over again

Some days I totally feel like giving up
For a direction I don't know where to turn
Understanding is all I want sometimes
A closer walk with my Savior I yearn

And when things seem most hopeless
Looking around I see no way out
My soul, mind, and body I place in his hand
My inner man questioning, "shout!"

And resting only on Jesus
And relying on him and not man
I continue to pray fervently through the storms of life

Looking to Jesus
A deep breath
And I stand

Written by: Tressa Ann Olden

A Cry for Help

Lord Jesus right now I'm needing your touch
I feeling this sadness I need you so much
This life with its circumstance I feel so much pain
I know holding to you there is much to gain.

I'm trying hard to fit in, but I still feel alone
I don't feel the love for me
On the cross that was shown

I'm tossing and turning, still trying to find an answer
Not trivial debates about being a dancer
I want to find in me, what's truly in you
As you walked this earth and taught us what to do

I want the dept, that you took to the grave
Reaching beyond
Assurance my soul is save

I can't move beyond, until you let me go
I need your guidance within me to flow
Please help me Lord to get through this pain
For without you Lord I'd surely go in sane

And daily I pray to get some relief
I need you to carry me
Through this world that brings grief

Content is where I want to be
But right now, I'm so far from it
Peace I plead right here on earth
Until you call me home by the trumpet

Written By: Tressa Ann Olden

Counting

There is something's I can count on
Tomorrow isn't one
That belongs to God himself
And his begotten son

He wakes me up in the morning
He starts me on my way
He's in control of all tomorrows
But right now, I'll use his given "TODAY"

Written by Tressa Ann Olden

At Peace?

Today is a very happy day
Nothing special but at peace with yourself
What you need to happen in your life real soon
Seems hopelessly sitting somewhere on a shelf

When you try and try and try some more
But things still go the same
You hope for something positive
Though life continues to throw you out of the game

You wait and wait to hear a word
You need encouragement too
Sometimes you feel like giving up
You can't say what you'd do

But today you're at peace you're all alone
If you don't ask no one will turn you down
You can for the moment enjoy yourself
Until the next time life hands you a frown

Written by: Tressa Ann Olden

Be Real

I wish your love was like Jesus's love, but honestly, I know that it ain't

You try to look beyond the faults but humanistic-ly you really can't

Jesus's love hides a multitude of faults of which He took to the
cross and died

We smile and embrace each other daily but our actions in love
does subside

We talk the talk but few walk the walk

But say we're going to heaven anyhow

We live today, like there's no tomorrow

And enjoy all the pleasures for now

But I do believe, He's coming back to His people

Whether water emerged or sprinkled

Every eye shall see Him, and every tongue shall confess

Back to a church; without spot or wrinkle.

Written by: Tressa Ann Olden

God Speaks Through His Creation

In the beginning God created the heaven and the earth

Genesis 1:1

Disappointed again

I could be angry, as I sit here this morning, finding myself in this state
Thinking of the reason, some people are mean,
Is strictly because of hate

I know from living, there is good in the world, though often I'm pressed to find it
My heart and soul reach out to those like me
Very few; but I stand behind it

Disappointed once again, don't know or realize, why so bitter the hate
It lands on whom it wants at anytime
Most often it seals our fate.

What I need, is out there somewhere, I need God's guidance on every step
I know He has something just for me
For his promises I have kept

Written by: Tressa Ann Olden

Don't cry

Don't cry for me I have gone to a better place
Don't cry for me I have finished the Christian race
I'm out of this world with its sorrow and its pain
Rejoice for me now a crown of gold I have gained
Don't cry for me now, He has allowed me heavenly rest
Don't cry for me now, I've finished life's test
He called me home He needed another soldier
Some He called younger me a little older
In life we are promised three score and ten
But only God knows when our life will end
Don't cry for me now, I'm standing by gates that are pearly
I fought a good fight, I finished the course, God loved me and brought me in early

Written by: Tressa Ann Olden

Everyone

It's been a long, long time
Since my savior went to the cross
We live today because of his love
To redeem us he paid the cost

He came down from heaven
For every one of us
Jesus has no respect of persons
So, there is no need to fuss

Black, white brown yellow
Gods' skin has not color
He hung there for each one of us
So, in him our lives will be fuller

He's God and there is no doubt about it
His love extends to us all
He now sitting at the right hand of the father
He awaits to hear our call

Written by Tressa Ann Olden

Fleeing

Here and now is here now
My! How the times does fly
A blink of an eye
A twist of the head
And the "now" soon passes by

Written by Tressa Ann Olden

I Believe

I believe that Jesus went to the cross unblemished just for me
I believe he suffered helplessly to set the sinner free
I believe he forgives all our sins and loves us through the fault
And God's only son's shed his blood and through it I was bought

Written by: Tressa Ann Olden

THE NEXT FOUR POEMS ARE PERSONALITY TRAITS. WHICH ONE ARE YOU?

1. *Director*
2. *Fun Seeker*
3. *Observer*
4. *Feeler*

Here are poems I have written in a series of four poems. These poems deal with traits of people. There are four main categories in which a person's personality fall into. And often time opposites attract. This poem is entitled "Observer". The other three in my series are entitled "Director", "Feeler" and "Fun-seeker".

Observer- one who is quiet by nature, is content just being a part of, usually intelligent but not out spoken, loves alone time.

Director- one who has leadership abilities and loves it, Will always speak up to be noticed when participating in a group activity, is outgoing, loves meeting and talking with people, sets high standards for his or herself, meticulous in attire, stands very tall in a crowd.

Feeler- one who takes everything and everyone as their assignment in keeping peace, very caring, logical, trustworthy, dependable, self-sacrificing, and very high maintenance.

Fun-seeker- very outgoing, the life of the party, lives for the moment, optimistic, very forgiving, is his own cheering section, unreliable, but very compassionate.

Director

Why am I made to feel like a second-class citizen?
When my accomplishments are second to none
I have been blessed with a wonderful job
I'm not boring I love to have fun.

My clothes I buy are top fashion,
My shoes are the latest style
My opinion of me is of the highest esteem
Just sit and talk with me for a while

It's not that I'm trying to get sympathy
That sure does not fit me at all
In a crowd I can certainly hold my own
I'm not lost I stand very tall

My standards for me are the highest
I'm ahead or two above the rest
Have one conversation a minute with me
I'll certainly pass the test

So why when my day is ended
And the sun no longer shines
that with everything I have in my life
Fulfillments not what I find

By day I'm happy and pleased with me
But within of truth there's a void
I read in my bible daily
That my help rests in the Lord.

And before the night has ended
Didn't wait another day
I found a place of quite comfort
And I began to pray

Well as I said I am an intellect
You don't have to tell me twice
So, I asked and today I share with you all
I use my God's advice.......

Written by: Tressa Ann Olden   2004

Fun Seeker

I'm living for this moment right now right here today
I'm loyal and exciting in every imaginable way

I'm told I bring life to the party
I keep everyone on the edge
I'm very optimistic in relationships
Often finding myself on a ledge

I am one who is very forgiving
All a part of my person they say
But holding on to problems is not one of my traits
For that was yesterday

My nature is totally charismatic
I bring my own cheering section hip hooray
I've crossed the line so many times
To say what I'm going to say

Unreliable, I'm busy I forgot
You certainly can't expect me to remember
I know what I did this morning
You're talking to me about last September

But do love me for all the compassion I bring
All my changes day to day won't be a bore
There is pleasure in loving a person like me
Are you willing to open the door?

Written By: Tressa Ann Olden

Observer

You are sort of and odd fellow
That's how my first encounter would go
But talk with me for a moment on any subject
And the truth will surely show.

I can do without the limelight
I'm content just being in the crowd
The accomplishments that are in my life'
by themselves they speak very loud.

I am often called a recluse
Simply because in a crowd hardly visible at all
But if you converse with me one on one
I'll talk you up a wall

Please don't insult my intelligence
Of this I get quickly offended
But as gentle of a person as you will meet
Forgiving so all hearts are mended

I excel I'm an over achiever
In temperament not easily huffed
And I feel just fine in casual clothes
No bother if shoes are scuffed

If you hear me in a crowd and I'm speaking
It's as much of a surprise to me to
That God uses all of us differently
And without warning he uses me instead of you

Written By: Tressa Ann Olden

Feeler

Why do I feel it is my assignment?
To keep peace all over this land
I often times go to the end of the world
To make one understand

I realize that if you do some things
Everything else will fall into line
I'm very caring, logical and trustworthy
And in temperament I am sublime

To most I appear melancholy
I over analyze, feeling layers are very thin
But my love for mankind is consistent
And I'm spirit filled from within

I love to create out of nothing
What God has placed here for me
Self-sacrifice when giving to others
And dependable as one can be

Some say I'm a little over sensitive
Philosophical, high maintenance to name a few
But the high standards that I place on myself
Most assuredly benefit you.

Understanding, great listener, sympathy to needs
Here I am God's design, God's pleasure
Hold me close be there for me when I need you
You will find in me a wondrous treasure

Written by: Tressa Ann Olden

Gap

Jesus took on a human form
To redeem the man of sin
Guiltless and blameless he went to the cross
So that man might live again

Now He intercedes for our thoughts
He knows the language of each groan
He petitions to the father on our behalf
Sitting beside him on the heavenly throne

When our prayers go up to heaven
He uncovers them like taking off a mask
And interprets each one to his father
For so often we don't know what to ask

I'm so glad He is there intervening
For we are his and he does understand
For when sin was abounding no hope for anyone
He stood in the gap for man

Written by Tressa Ann Olden

Not alone

They grew up not really knowing

Just what life had in store
The God of this universe
"Who we reverence, respect and adore

This young boy had no idea
When he became a man
That God would send him far from
home with a rifle in his hand.

He who knows all, must surely know
this young man with a gun
Left behind a loving family
A wife, a mom a son
He got the call, and boarded a plane
To follow his enlisted orders
He soon realized he was not alone
There were many moms,
sisters and daughters.
They willing gave to their country
For our freedom they gave up their right
To stay home with their families and be
sent far away to fight.

We pray every day for their safety
We pray God's protection on them
That news we hear will find them safe
Good news, not something that's grim

So, we're placing them in your hands Lord
Asking that you bring them safely back home
We want their families to know we are praying
Let them know they're not alone

Written by: Tressa Ann Olden   2004

Remembering 9/11   2001

911 the day the world stood still for many
Grief stricken were those and lost lives were plenty
So many tears and so much sadness loneliness indelible pain
Terrorist hating, lying and cheating
You think who in heaven or on earth is to blame.

So many lost their daughters, young children left alone
To a world with hate that took precious loved ones
Wives lost their husbands, children lives just beginning
And grief-stricken fathers their sons

Our hearts are so heavy with grief in this nation
With bitterness, and the sadness we all had to face
We watched heavyhearted people running and screaming
Trying hopelessly to find a hiding place.

Some are still asking why God allowed this awful thing
Tragedy that struck the towers and the planes
Left are memories that are vivid in our minds forever
We live over and over again.

So many things happen in life we often search to understand
But take rest on the fact that God's in control
Though tragic were the thousands of people whose lives were lost
God knows them all and many were written on His role

Written By: Tressa Ann Olden

The Grove

The weather was perfect for golfing
Up early brisk morning sunlight
A get away is something we needed
We were here and everything was all right

The scenery that surrounded the course
Was breathtaking to say the least
The windblown trees with artistic shapes
A painter's broad scope would be eased

The white sandy beaches along coastal blue water
Rugged rocks extend your eye to the edge
A gull flying overhead
A crow flying by
A deer standing motionless not afraid

The cool breeze off the ocean
The view picturesque
Who could ask for a better place to be?
We certainly enjoyed our time together
Every moment My hubby and me

Written by: Tressa Olden

God Speaks through other people

"And He gave some prophets; and some evangelists; and some pastors and teachers,"

Ephesians 4:11

The women

God spoke so boldly to us from his written word. Each passage read or spoken by the women came from His inspired obedient men who left it on record for us as an example to follow. The services were intense and purpose driven by the Holy Spirit. Tears flowed freely to lose those shackled in their past bondages. Some were dumb found to see God moving and working in the lives of so many of the women. Many of us were moved to another place in our spiritual walk and a few were awestruck about just how wonderful He really is! 'He, "God" allowed us to step out of self and become one with Him. Moving into the newness of Jesus Christ where we found rest for our weary souls. He laid for us a foundation of which to build on. We were purged, cleanse and renewed by the power that only comes from on high. And we reverenced the only true and living God. As we refreshed ourselves in Jesus Christ we were reminded over and over again of His mercy, His forgiveness and assured of His love for each of us. We made new friendships, renewed old friendships and built lasting relationships to help strengthen our heart, mind and body with God and one another. We left hurt, disappointments, anger, bitterness and pain behind and step into healing and forgiveness of ourselves as well as others receiving a total reinsurance in our Savior and His promises. God truly spoke to us women through His chosen women of God who did not dilute His word nor sugar coat it to align with our feelings. They read it and said it and taught it in a way to be understood by all who sat and listened to the voice of Jesus as He spoke through them. We rejoiced knowing that He was in that place of total control each time we met. And at His feet I lay every situation presented. I was blessed beyond measure! How about you?

Written by: Tressa Ann Olden

A Country Stroll

One day I took a walk on a long country road
The once traveled path laced with a wall of pine
trees along its sides extending for miles; was now showing patches
of grass growing through the dust of years gone by.

Pinecones, pebbles and rocks of all shapes and sizes tossed about
along the way as the now less frequented traveled trail
turn further into the clearing of the woods

The Bald Cypress trees spread out as if touching
to hold each other made a covering of shade from the
afternoon sun. A large lone oak tree set in the middle
of a clearing with wild branches of muscadine vines
entwine at the base, holding many childhood memories

Beautiful white Magnolia blossoms stood in a patch of
ground near a shabby little house with a large porch
supported by two pillars at each end.

Walking on, I spotted in the distance, a lake where crawdads
could be caught on a string and tossed in a bucket, with a
little luck and some patience a mess of catfish could be caught
for the night's supper. The rope marks left on the big tree from
swinging high touching the branches
A barbwire fence now replaced laughter with a sign warning danger.

Suddenly at the roads end stood this once bigger than life
white wooden house with its tall steps and large porch
a white picket fence, long chains hanging connected to support a
swing that swayed back and forth screeching loudly.

The quaint little screen door that kept out the mosquitoes as
we ran in and out to get a large glass of homemade lemonade
on a hot summer's day

Years passed before my eyes; things appeared so much smaller as I stood
looking at the big block of wood where I stood to hold the old water pump handle that
needed to be primed and holding the rusting bent silver dipper in my hand, I could get a cool
drink of water.

Once beautiful fields of okra, watermelons, and pecan trees
now showed tall blades of grass growing wildly toward the sky.
The old horse saddle draped across the rickety fence was frayed
from many a winters weather. Birds had built a nest in the large old
wagon bed, the weight of the handle alone would knock you down

The bright red shiny tractor faded to a pale orange and the
rusty plow that set near it was covered with woven webs of
a spider giving way to absence of usage since its earlier days.

I stood there for a moment still, AND REMEMBERED

Written by: Tressa Ann Olden   2004

A Daily Walk with Jesus

A daily walk with Jesus
Is one we must employ?
A daily walk with Jesus
Brings our wanting soul much joy

A daily walk with Jesus
Will guide our every step
A daily walk with Jesus
Is one we must accept?

For he made us in His Image
He fashioned us with His love
He created us to honor Him
And pleased His father with the descending of a dove

Written by: Tressa Ann Olden   2004

The Garden

As I began to walk through a garden of flowers, "behold what a garden!"

At the back was the beautiful Morning Glory's, standing near the entrance welcoming all who entered. Little Sweet Peas were scatter about snuggling under a larger flower that was near them, seemingly knowing they were related.

Every garden as its own section of Snapdragons, that as potential to be beautiful but brings discontentment and cause problems. The very large Sunflowers towering high above the rest showing off their leadership abilities within their row stood still. The whimsical small Pansies smiled delightfully greeting each one as they passed by while a bunch of Sweet Williams sang devotional hymns of praise. The Fiddleneck and Claret-Cup Cactus played on instruments softly as to not disturb the mood of the moment.

I moved a little closer an heard the Lily of the Valley and the, Bleeding Hearts, praying out loud to the most High under what appear to a Weeping Willow.

The Christmas rose sat silently remembering His birth, the winter snow God's gift to all kind. So many Gladiolus, Tulips, and Daffodils showing off the large hats of their heads fashioned in brilliant colors. I looked again to see an Orange bunch of Touch-Me-Not's daring to move from their seats for fear of losing them to the family of Showy Gaillardia entering the door.

The Bright Flame Azalea and the Tea Rose with its vibrant sparkle, made up the front rows near the podium while down the other side the Big-leaved Hydrangea, and the Lilac embraced the Bridal wreath that stood with the Rose of Sharon. Directly behind it was a large arrangement of mums, which made up the angelic choir with voices that hummed a holy melody.

Flying high in the spirit was the Bird-of Paradise that had stop to hold a conversation with the African violet regarding an upcoming meeting that week.

It all came together as the Tall Bearded Iris introduced the Crown Imperial to the Congregation. Behold the Garden............

Written By: Tressa Ann Olden   2004

God Speaks

Don't just listen to what God has to say; hear Him

He that hath an ear, let him hear what the Spirit saith...

Revelations 3:13

Boxcar Experience

One day I stood in a choir stand that reflected being in

a boxcar. With capabilities to move left and right I tried standing

virtually still but it became next to impossible. Many times, moving swiftly

I was thrown against the sides with little to hold on to which made being

tossed from east to west easy. Boxcar choir design does not allow as much movement back and forth as side-to-side. Moving quickly about there is never enough time that your footing is ever secure. Only confined within the walls of a small space you are limited in where you go or move. Keep praying for He spoke to a turbulent sea (peace be still.) Continuing on with no firm, secure grip only trusting the door that held me in could not slide or swing open on its own you rest knowing that God will never leave you or forsake you. Then all of a sudden it stops, it's over, and you check bruises and scars, but after taking a deep breath you realize (life) The door is opened, (by the one who opens doors that are closed in our face) Your eyes are looking up to the hills from which cometh Strength............

Written By: Tressa Ann Olden

Change

What makes me who I am? this is a question I ask myself
Book after book I read to find answers to have them just
collecting dust on the shelf

My personality the things I do are all a part of by being
Though the thing that really defines you I am
That's the part I am puzzled with seeing

He gave to us these unique attributes, so many of us not one the same. From head to toe he's
fashioned us aligning often only in name.

From birth He gave us His image
And likeness that reflects who He is
Standards set from His father above
From the dust He formed us to be His

He placed in us a free will those choices
in life which to make
what path will give me the answers
which road in life should I take.

If I want to be more like Jesus,
The example the pattern He gave
Reading and studying His written word
Placing deep in my heart there to save

Yes, I want to be just like Jesus
There are surely some things I must do
He has given in His word, some powerful tools
That refresh, restore and renew

So today as I look over my life
Where I am is a bit out of range
If I want to be more like my Savior
The life I have left I must change

Written by: Tressa Ann Olden

Company's coming

Clean up clean up company's coming
Clean up the living room
Make sure that things are in order
Our company will be here soon.

Don't worry that your closet's untidy
Don't bother arranging your shoes
The one who is coming accepts who you are
He does not follow society's rules

He does not come looking on the outside
He concerns himself only what's within
If we allow Him on the inside
The outside itself will amend

I've done something's I am so worried
I'm drab, look at me, I'm a bore
I repeat it again, no concern to Him
Be quiet now He's knocking at your door

Okay, uncomfortable but here I am
Many things still left for me to do
But I'm willing to let Him in right now
You said in Him I can renew

Dear Jesus I stand before you nervous
Asking forgiveness for all things that are wrong
I have lost countless battles with this flesh of mine
I've heard you will make me strong

Here I go I'm walking to the door
One last check to make sure all's in place
I see my Savior standing on the outside
I'm staring Him right in the face

What's next, what's next to do?
I've cleaned the best I can
Reached out, confess and believe with your heart
He's knocking "Just let Him in

Written By: Tressa Ann Olden

Sweet Spirit

Her voice illuminates the room, the pain the hurt the sadness the gloom

Sweet spirit

The notes of healing feel the air, God answers but a fervent prayer,

Sweet spirit

Up the scales, not one is missed, as if each has been touched, with an angelic kiss

Sweet spirit

Her song she sang, is loud and clear, her inner strength, He holds her near

Sweet spirit

What the heavenly Father does with her song, mending hearts as they come along

Sweet spirit

Give your heart to God, she sang one day, as wayward sinners found their way

Sweet spirit

In her palm He placed to pen, lyrics that reach the soul and heart of men,

Sweet spirit

God's gift to her, was His to give, He breathes on her and lets us live HIS SWEET SPIRIT

Written by; Tressa Ann Olden   2003

Glad

I'm glad that God surely knows me
He knows the thoughts in my mind
When words I think should flow so free
With mouth formed there are no words I find

My heart is full of what to say
Most often working overtime
For when it comes to speaking out
Most words seemed so refine

But concerns of the heart
Are ones that matter most
God has a way of letting me rest
Under His great edge I boast

He allows me time to think it through
I know He cares for me
He carried the cross and bore the stripes
That I might be set free

And so, I stand with trembling heart
Whenever I need to speak
He always shows up right on time
When this flesh I'm in gets weak.

Written by: Tressa Ann Olden

Bethlehem, Calvary, Jerusalem

In a manger in Bethlehem our savior was born
For the inn said the innkeeper "there's no room

On a cross at Calvary where He gave up His life
His dead body wrapped, carried and laid in a borrowed tomb

But thank God for Jerusalem on the third day He rose
And brought life with His victory over death and the grave

He paid the ultimate price for the sins of mankind
And bought forgiveness to every human's headed
gloom.

Written by: Tressa Ann Olden

I Ain't

You never ever encourage me
You constantly say I can't
You put me down every chance you get
And tell me what I ain't

I tell you that I trusting God!
You're forever asking me why
I tell you that he's by my side
You say why do you cry

Sometimes I don't know where to
go to get the break I need
I'll trust in God my head up high
Dear God help me I plead

So now I stand right in your face
Ignoring what you say and do
Putting me down won't build you up
and I ain't "studdin" you!

Written By: Tressa Ann Olden   2004

I came

I came here broken hearted
I came bitter in soul
I came disappointed
But I came

I came discouraged
I came sadden from fear
I came bewildered
But I came

In this state I found Jesus
In this state I surely found Love
Though the outlook was anything but instant
I continue to seek Gods guidance from above

I am visibly not where He wants me
I'm am ever so close to Him now
Each day I step eagerly toward Him
Trusting He is my answer to how?

I thought about waiting to come differently
I wanted to be better to come
Though He accepted all of my brokenness
And placed a melody in my heart to hummmmm

I come to Him now giving thanks,
for everything I have been through
For He controls my every movement
bidding all past failures adieu

I came one day not knowing
If tomorrow was worth going through
But Jesus walks with me and cares for me
And loves me like His painted sky blue..........

Written By: Tressa Ann Olden

I Claim

Why do you always put me down?
When I'm striving to do my best

I may not live up to your standards
Or even pass your test

But God has made me in is image
From my mother he gave me birth

My father has been right by my side
From the day I was conceived on this earth

Don't make me anything but who I am
Putting me down doesn't benefit you
God as uniquely fashioned us differently
He restores, refreshes us new

So, pray and take time to know me
I'm God's and he loves me just the same
I may not live up to your standards for me
But in Jesus the victory I claim.

Written By Tressa Ann Olden   2004

I-t, impossible things

Impossible things are not of Jesus
For there is nothing impossible with God
He led Moses and the children of Egypt to the deep Red Sea
And parted it with only a rod

He took two fish and five loaves of bread
And fed the multitude
And met a woman at Jacob's well
With living water, she was renewed

A blind man received his sight
With Jesus anointing him with spittle and clay
And allowed his disciple Peter to walk on water
If only for a day

He put a ram in the bush
For brother Abraham to find
And such a gracious guest was he
Turned water into wine

He called a boy named David
And put three stones in his hand
Who slew the giant ten times his size?
While under His command

He also had Joshua's army
To march around and around
With shouts and praises and believing in God
The Jericho walls came down

He called out Lazarus from the grave
And gave Saul of Troas a new name
And laid on brother Noah to build an ark
And by two the animals entered the same

Nothing is impossible with Jesus
If in him you would only believe
For he takes us through the valley of death
In order that we might achieve
        Faith

Written By. Tressa Ann Olden

Love

To love someone is not always easy
It's the hardest thing some folk have ever done
To love those even our enemies
God demonstrated by sending His son

Love those who falsely accuse you and
And the ones you ostracize your name
Jesus said in following me love them
for too me they did exactly the same

Love, because that's who I am
Love, let the heavenly bells ring
Love lifted me when nothing else could
Love is a beautiful thing

Written by: Tressa Ann Olden   2004

Megafest: Atlanta GA. 2004

June 23-26 Georgia Dome, Phillips Arena

I came here to Megafest to find a closer applicable walk with Jesus Christ. One that does not compromise my true belief in Jesus himself and one that teaches me not to judge anyone by outward appearances. I pray for a walk with Christ that allows me to get to know people and their story. And to let God alone judge each and every situation. I choose to treat people the way I would like to be treated and to share Christ with all mankind. I always put forth an effort to be careful of how I talk or entertain a stranger or any person I meet. Whether I encounter them day to day or every now and then I must treat them with respect like you're meeting for the first time, for Gods' angels are everywhere even in the circus.

I have learned over my life to adhere to leadership that always exemplifies God through a Godly quality and actions. That shows itself daily in their outward vision as they follow Jesus Christ. I also have come to a realization that change is needed in order to be what God wants from each of us. Change of mind, change of body and a change of outlook every day. We must die daily from weights that keep us from helping someone. Weights of hatred, envy, maliciousness, jealousy and pride that cause us to be useless to everyone. We must receive power, endured from on high and not by our own self-pride be powerless. But let us step out boldly before God and man sharing what he has given us little or much and watch the increase in our lives. We must not continue to live defeated lives wondering about Gods will for us. We must study his word daily and take back the stuff that has been promised to us through his word. We must continue to resist Satan and lay claim to what he has taken from us as God's children. REALIZING THAT IT ALL BELONGS TO GOD. Stand on Gods promises, not wavering but firmly planting our feet with his written word. Knowing that it will not return void but through Jesus Christ it will accomplish. AMEN

Tressa Ann Olden

Mirror

I looked into a reflection
It was broken, disappointed and I felt despair
Confused, bitter and discouraged and had scattered
Pieces that seem to go nowhere

I looked and some pieces seemed larger some smaller
arranging in size
I tried forming something that resembled a smile
But ultimately took on a disguise

As I looked again, I could see, that the mirror wasn't
shattered at all
It was the image it reflected and the shadowed likeness
of a silhouette on the bedroom wall

This likeness of me had come to this,
oh, just what has happened to me?
The sparkle the confidence the image
Once had was lifeless and withdrawn
As can be.

I stood for a moment in silence knowing well,
But still unsure and in disbelief
The smooth polished surface that was in front of me
Looked back with nothing but grief.

No matter what direction I turned in it
It mocked the same gesture
Even when I put my best clothes on
The mirror would only fester

I looked around within the place that held
Only me
And began to talk out loud to God
The one I could not see

I told him that I was a broken vessel
and hurting deep in my soul
I know you sent your darling Son
That I might be made whole.

I stand here now all torn to pieces
With tears streaming down my face
I need a healing touch from you
My life is a disgrace

All of a sudden without any notice
I found my knees on the floor
I cried out loud and ask the Lord
To come in and restore

And piece-by-piece life comes together
One-day one-step at a time
He's healing the reflection that mirrors me
And allows His brilliance to shine

Written by: Tressa Ann Olden   2004

107

Perfect

Perfect no one but Jesus he is the only one
Virgin born from his mother's womb in a manger is life begun

He left heaven and came in this world that we might have eternal life
Not to condemn the sinner man whose life is filled with strife?

Encourage one another, uplift if you can, don't speak ill of anyone's fault
Just love them as the bible says, and be an example with your life and walk.

No sin is greater than any other whether lying, drinking, or to fornicate.
God dislikes the sin not the sinner he says we must love and not hate

Assemble yourself with believers that's what the bible says to do
When faced with grumbling and talking about one another it doesn't help your spirit renew

Forgive one another over and over, it's a lesson that we all must learn
For Jesus himself left ninety and nine to find the one of great concern

Reach out beyond what you're use to, give it your all, be patient with a lot
You will find strength in obeying God, if you're willing to give all you've got

And remember no one is perfect, we're all sinners saved by grace
God sent his son as an example to all, in helping us run this race

Perfect, you say, keep thinking, I know not a single one
Though God loved us enough to let us know our soul rest within His Son.

Perfection is only found in Jesus, and Jesus Christ alone
Ask him to create in you a clean heart, that will meet him one day at the throne

Writen by Tressa Ann Olden

Pianist

The melody echoed all through the ears
Of all who sat in that place
The sweet sound of music a gift that He gave
Transcending a heavenly embrace

As each note was played, the marquee would read
"The Greatest Pianist I've heard"
She sat and commanded each note key by key
Listener's hearts deep inside were stirred

What visions were shared as she played on and on
Giving all of herself to this piece
Crescendos ranging that varied the scales
No one hurried the performance to cease

A chosen vessel miraculous and beautiful
God is wonderful to share His gift He gave
The spirit moved mightily throughout that room
Her gift of music caused souls to be saved

Written By: Tressa Ann Olden

Prayer

Prayer is very essential
Meaning it is something that we all need
Daily we must walk and talk to Him
And His written word we must take heed.

There is nothing that we cannot tell Him
There isn't anything that we can't entrust
He admonishes us to bring it to Him
For His spirit does dwell with us

He is direction for those who need to find their way
He is peace in this confused land
He's a friend when you are feeling all alone
He is help when you need a hand

No matter what situation you find yourself
No matter how far you have gone
Jesus Christ does forgive all of our faults
Price was paid on His way to the throne

So don't be ashamed to pray to Him
Don't let anyone stop your request
Jesus as the power to make wrong things right
Believe me! He knows what is best.

Now do take a moment with my Savior
Make it personal He belongs to us all
He is waiting ever patience for your presence
When's the last time you've given Him a call?

Written by: Tressa Ann Olden   2004

Pre soak

Pre-soak is part of the cleaning process
Pre-soak is part of the plan
As we are washed and cleansed in the word of God
To ultimately help us stand

Pre-soak is a dying daily
Of sins that befall all of us
The stains of life that weight us down
Through Jesus Christ we are found just

We cannot hurry His purposes
But should entrust them in God's hand
He knows our every waking hour
He is in total command

As His we must wait on Him
He knows all of what we need
Heed His instructions and wait on His time
For in doing, we will succeed

Study as he tells us in Timothy
Learn of Him take up His yoke
We will rejoice with HIM one day
If with patience while in pre-soak

God Bless Megafest 2004
Tressa Ann Olden

Rainbow

When I started this life in Jesus there were things I didn't understand;
He admonished me to continue on he'd be there on command
From day to day there were ups and downs often bleak and gray;
Hold on my child every storm as an end trust God for a brighter day

Ostracized, lied on and mocked because in this walk, we're peculiar and set apart;
Visions of my savior's death on the cross, the price he paid for our sins with blood he bought.

Rainey days that have no end we asked how long; thinking this battle is yours to fight my
child you're wrong; Wind and turmoil twist and turns we're upside down; Constant grief
and pain in Satan's clutches we are bound.

But my child I have you securely in my hands; Though confusion now is controlling all your
plans; In this world we are lost in Jesus we are found; So be still and know your stand is
solid ground.

Soon swaying and leaning have slowed down it has ceased I can smile; I am continuing on in
Jesus every step every mile; Going through the storms with him holding my trembling hand;
Some days are rough to take while others spectacular and grand; But at the core the storm
comes to the end; you step out on faith and substance does began. As you continue on looking
upward to the sky GOD PLACES A RAINBOW………

Written By: Tressa Ann Olden

Sister's

Instinctively we love out loud
We learned to share everything with one another
We always took care that nothing came between us
And played every day with each other

We grew

We share, but not everything
We're there whenever if you need me
We still see or talk often as we choose
Lives lived don't always agree

Life changes

But love shared instinctively is unconditional
We're Sister's

Tressa Ann Olden   2004

The look of things

Things sure don't look like there suppose to
Haven't turned out like I thought they should
Jesus Christ was sent to save the world
Is what I understood

Things that have been established
To help the poor and in need
Are going to enhance the riches wants
And those already in greed

Why God we find ourselves asking
Have you let this come to pass?
He said my child be anxious for nothing
For troubles don't always last

I came that men may be set free
They put thorns on my head
I healed their sick and fed 5000
On a cross they rendered me dead

Many counted me out as they looked at the nails
The place where I gave up my life
But I rose from the dead in spite of their thoughts
And gave victory to those in strife

So don't be discouraged, don't be dismayed
Trust in God for He is in it
He says He would never leave us alone
As I study, I know that He meant it.

Tressa Ann Olden   2004

The Seed

The word of God is like a seed
It has potential to grow.
If fertilized and tilled just right
The plant will surely show

It starts out down under the dirt
Where only the water can reach
The roots will form the plant will sprout
The word of God will teach

You began by digging through each scripture
Like the soil sometimes very hard
Plant in your mind that continuing
brings to you a great reward

Fertilize by studying the bible
To be approved the word does say
Water it diligently with a fervent prayer
And read it each and everyday

Written by: Tressa Ann Olden   2004

This Man

There is no reason to doubt this man
who died for our sins?
He bought our life with His shed blood
And let us live again

Nothing before could set us free
Though Priest and rams sure tried
The son was sent "the lamb of God"
Unblemished on the cross he died

He hung nailed hands two thieves by His side
Blood beaten by His accuser's whip
His feet bore nails, a sword pierced side
Anyone else would have given them lip

But the man on the cross who stood in the gap
Asked forgiveness for their sins and mine
For He knew His death would bring us life
If in Him we would only incline

He finished the task that He came here for
The bitter cup that could not pass
In Him we find eternal life
Understanding, unspeakable to grasp!

Written By: Tressa Ann Olden   2004

To Accomplish

How He must have felt to accomplish
Just what he set out to do
God's son of this great universe
Spoke these words on the cross for me and you

He came as an innocent child
Lowly born in a manger He lay
Rode in on a donkey in His mother's womb
No room in the Inn for them to stay

At age twelve He left his father and mother
To do what God the father placed in His heart
He traveled around teaching God's mercies
And a study of God's word to impart

After confronting and defeating the devil
He gave us victory and a way we must live
Let the written scripture live within your heart
And don't be ashamed of it but offer and freely give

Praying fervently prayers to the Father
Without a fight he gave up His right
To be mocked and whipped though still innocent
In a court they accused and tried him all night

But for you and me He took every lash
Till His blood hit the dirt from which we came
On the cross where they nailed him and pierced his side
"Our father", he called out his name

Forgive them is one thing that was spoken
As he closed his eyes and gave up the ghost
Its FINISHED words spoken as he bowed his head
That's proof He loved us MOST

Written by Tressa Ann Olden

To know

I know that Jesus loves me, I know he really cares
All thoughts and concerns within my life
He lets me know he shares

He never lets my weights, get heavier than I can bear
He's with me every step of the way
Though not always knowing He's there!

Even when life seems hopeless, I turn my thoughts to him
In every situation that seem endless
With circumstances seemingly grim

Jesus gives me joy, only He can understand
I keep my thoughts on him a lone
He's always in command

And though all around me, my world is falling down
Jesus gives me peace of mind you see
Where no peace came be found.

Written By: Tressa Ann Olden

True Friend

Was it greed that betrayed my Jesus?
Was it hatred that nailed Him to the cross?
Is it unconfessed sin of all mankind that
cause our soul to be loss

He is the keeper of hearts
He is the restorer of the soul
He promises to never leave us alone
In Him we are made whole

I can pray to him daily for my needs
He gives peace to my mind
He forgives my every fault indeed
He's a true friend you will find

He cared so much for us
to rise from the dead
early on that third day morning
he rose just like he said

He went up with His father
To prepare a place for me
So, has I lived this life on earth
I am victoriously

He lets me walk and talk with Him
And daily I understand
Jesus Christ our Savior
Was truly God and truly man

Written By: Tressa Ann Olden

120

Vine

The vineyard took on the appearance of beautiful laced doily
draped over an open green field. Each individual vine with its pointed
leaves, entwined in what seemed to be sculptured branches that stood close to each other
making a straight row from end to end in both directions

It's no wonder nature brings forth canvas prints that can and is enjoyed by
all, simply stop and observe it. The green leaves against the open sky
with brown stems never ending, fused against the ash bronze dirt that covers God's earth, is
to one breathless. Heaven knows the fruit of those vines are
gathered in baskets by bunches that are hanging from the waiting vine until harvest. Each
bunch triangles from bottom to top with a flowing motion resembling ornaments of a
Christmas tree

Again, the hand of God shines its bright sunshine through the fruit allowing
the sweetness to enter each tiny individual grape. Kissing it ever so gently
as not to harm its outer layer, that covers the juice in its center.
I am the vine, ye are the branches

Written by: Tressa Ann Olden

What's in a name?

There is power in His name
There is peace in His name
There is joy unspeakable
In His name

His name brings assurance
His name is light
His name is Jesus
Jesus is His name

Written by: Tressa Ann Olden

Why

Why am I made to feel unworthy?
When God says "not so"
Why do in mind I dream of places?
When there's no possible way to go

Could it be the limits I have
placed on myself
For God knows and has everything
He's always there to help

In Him there's no goal
That we cannot reach
In Him we can do all things,
the bible does teach

Do let Jesus Christ be the center your guide
Put away self-pity discard any pride
For greater things is written he says we will do
If in Him we rest, abide, and renew

Written By: Tressa Ann Olden   2004

Let go

I get so frustrated sometimes about the little things
What to me doesn't make a lot of sense
It's not that I asked for the world on a tray
But every now and then I look for recompense

I give until there is nothing left to give
My feelings, my heart openly
But many times, not expecting in return
I'm sadden and grieved as can be

But I'm going on and pushing through this pain
For its what life does all by itself
So again, I find myself all alone
And my feelings are sitting neatly on a shelf.

Written By: Tressa Ann Olden

Yoked

Yoked up to serve and worship Him
In all I do and say

Yoked up to lend a helping hand
Each and everyday

Yoked up to get a deeper meaning
Of the promises that He gives

Yoked up to finish the race I run
To live the life, He lives

So please don't be unequally yoked
But take His yoke and learn

No communion has light and darkness
Eternity or your soul will burn

Written by: Tressa Ann Olden

Compensation

We go through life's struggles so weary
We're tormented so often with stress
We strive every day to give all we have
And put forth our very, very best

So often we feel we're not appreciated
For all of the things that we do
It seems most times we're rejected
And our many accomplishes turn into few

We stop! Wanting to give what's in us
We stop wanting to give our all
We just want everyone to leave us alone
And want even answer when they call

Don't stop it's what they want from you!
Don't let them belittle your gift
Don't buy into bitterness about them either
But pray to God that your spirit will lift

So, walk on with your head up high
Your repayment is not here anyway
A much greater reward is waiting for you
If you don't buy into this world's today!

Written by: Tressa Ann Olden

Eden

In the garden was the tree of knowledge of good and evil
And Adam he assuredly walked with God
He had everything a man in this world could want
And with peace in every step his feet were shod

God was so very, very pleased with his Adam
Allowing him to name an animal of every kind
There was love, peace, and harmony among each one of them
All was well no sign of trouble you would find

And God said: it's good

He looked one day upon the man that he had made
And He said it's not right that he be alone
So, He laid him down in a deep, deep sleep
And from his side God took out a single bone

Man lay in a deep sleep, as God completed his work
Shaping and modeling another being in His hand
Some parts looked just like His first being Adam
A little softer, a lot gentler, so He called her WOMAN

And God said: it's good

How oh, how could this Garden of Eden get any better?
Adam asked as he looked upon his beautiful new bride
Birds were singing, flowers blooming, she was happy
Nothing alive was causing harm to any kind

Standing alone for a moment she was confronted by a persuasive snake
Out walking one fine day she happened upon the tree
Eat he said, from the tree, in the middle of the garden
And I declare you will know as much as He.

At that point she should have ran and still be running
But she stood and was overtaken by the lie
He's just telling you that, but you will know everything
You'll be smart, intelligent, wise, you won't die

One little bite, what's a bite it won't hurt?
This she reasoned with the tree's fruit in her hand
There I bit it, He won't know what I've done
I'll go to my husband Adam, he will surely understand

Adam! Adam taste of this delicious fruit
It won't hurt it will only make you smart
So, he took the fruit from her and did partake
And instantly he felt the shame in his heart

So, they ran so very deep into the garden
Trying to hide their naked bodies with fig leaves
Soon they heard the mighty voice of God calling
They now felt so guilty, like a robber or some thieves

Come out now He said and why are you both hiding?
Come out now and tell me exactly what you've done
Adam spoke quickly it was this woman you gave me Lord
But God said no, the fault lies with the one

For what you two have done I must banish you from this place
Your disobedience with the fruit has caused your fall
There is nothing you can do though you must leave now
And the consequences of your sin will lie on all

And from that day man was made to toil the ground
Woman's bearing years would bring her so much pain
And that mean conniving serpent was made to crawl on his belly
But their sin is lived over and over again

Written by: Tressa Ann Olden

God!

God, please allow me to talk with you a moment
Sometimes I feel so overwhelmed.
Why does it seem to me, that I'm so misunderstood?
Taken advantage of and needing your help.

I know of myself I can do nothing
I'm trying all I know to do what's right
Though it seems those that are closer to me
Put up battles and I constantly fight

I want to be who you made me to be
I can't be anyone else
I just want to serve you the best I know how
I read my bible it's not left on a self

Please God right now if you're listening
I know you know this is me!
You said our battles are not with flesh and blood
So, I ask now from this set me free!

Written by: Tressa Olden

Happiness

I feel so happy inside right now
My only wish is that this feeling would stay

It's not often life hands me a steady flow
I certainly don't want it to go away.

I strive hard not to let people or things get me down
I look constantly to the hills

Determine to keep my hand in His
I battle with this life and its thrills

When I am happy, it's not because
Of anything that I have done

My happiness comes from my Heavenly father
Who love me enough to send his only begotten Son

Written by Tressa Ann Olden

Life's tight places

To me my life is going rapidly downhill
I can't seem to succeed at a lot of things
I try with all the strength that's in me
But ultimately only failure it brings

With everything weighing I pull myself up again
Vowing to try and try it one more time
But every moment tends to put me back further
The spirit of my being I see decline

I'm stuck here in a tight place in my mind
I really don't know where to go
I feel I have no friend to turn to
My eyes filled with tears overflow

I keep looking and looking for a way out
I seek every way needing an escape
Won't someone please give me a chance at this thing?
Your successes I've tried hard to emulate

I see everyone succeeding all around me
Accomplishing their task and their goals
I ask myself over and over again
Why don't I fit into those roles?

I'm caught right now in a place
In my mind so small I need relief
I seem to be trying as hard as anyone
But this life is handing me nothing but grief

I hear stories that are very inspiring
Of failures that have turned to success
But it seems no matter what I lay on the table
It soon fades and is replaced by another's best

So dear God this is where I really am
Can't turn left, can't turn right up or down
I realize that if anything is accomplished in my life
It's in You and You only I have found

Everyday this place gets tighter and tighter
I get frustrated disappointed I just want to shout
But I have learned you are shaping and molding my life
To be content when it's time you will pull me out

Written By: Tressa Ann Olden

Questions

When will my miracle happen?
When will I get my break through?
When will the sorrows and hurt go away?
When will this heart of mine renew?

When will I be able to forgive?
When will I love my brother?
When will I be able to reach out and touch?
The heart the soul of another

When will I be set free?
When will all the guilt of past things fade?
When will I know that I'm free of sin?
WHEN WILL I STOP BEING AFRAID?

I asked these questions of my Savior
As I kneeled down at his feet fervently to pray
He's says the answers my child is abiding in me
Study your bible, to be approved everyday

Tressa Ann Olden   2005

134

Delight in the Lord

Psalms 37

Let's have some fun

Black Like Me

I remember the years of the fifties, sixties and seventies
This phrase was on everyone's lips
Narue jacket's, big Afros and platform shoes
Worn by everyone not just the very hip

Polka dots, flower patterns, Palazzo suits
They were making the scenes everywhere
Eight track tape, forty-five records, and initial blouses
And the theater movie blockbuster 'Hair"

Family outings, large gatherings, all day church
Gospel quartets, river baptism, all the mirth
Uncle Sam drafting, project living, sequence shirt
Muhammad Ali, Angela Davis, mini skirts

This was a thing of my life that was fun
And I rest in the fact that it's done
This was all part of growing I have earned
Not to do it anymore I have learned

Written By: Tressa Ann Olden

County Fair

What a jubilation it was at the county fair
Hundreds and hundreds of people moving everywhere
Water rides and rodeo ponies and stuffed animals
Corn dogs and cotton candy, I declare

Bumper cars and roller coaster's bumping and clanking
Ferris wheels so high in the sky that go round and round
Exhibits and farm animals some big some small
What kind of fair would it be without a clown?

Slides of every imaginable color going up and down
Balloons in the air all shapes and all sizes
Rock climbing and bungee jumping designed for all ages
And animated animals in many forms and disguises

What a day this was fun time well spent
but there is still much more for me to try
Mom and dad says can't do it all in one day
You look up and asked them so innocently
Why?

Golfing

The day I spent with my husband his choice of what to do
How's about we take in a game of golf, sounds great just me and you

We made our way to the golf course secured the game and cart
He got his clubs', put on his shoes to the greens is where we would start

I was there to lend a hand, and to keep him company
He played the game with other golfers who used their strategy

Honey, please bring me my putter, please mark the score on the card
The course it took some twist and turns and distance is measured in yards.

Drive the cart and press the brakes park underneath the shady tree
I'll use my driver to hit the ball accurately from the tee.

The course is very challenging the trees and water play a part
The stories they go on forever but he continued his game with heart

Bogie someone would shout, did you par another would ask?
Keeping the ball straight on the fairway to some is quite a task.

With conversations regarding family, children interest wives and work
There are even golfers who though total gentlemen are witty but somewhat a quirk

The day was very enjoyable I made it to the eighteenth hole
He played the game with confidence I watched each round unfold.

The game got a bit lengthy my patience with it grew thin
But for love I was determined to see it through all the way to the end.

The game was played for fun, no stress a leisure day out
He finished his game enjoyed himself and was happy that I didn't pout

Written by Tressa Olden   2004

Hot sauce please?

Thanksgiving Day is coming soon
The turkey will no longer strut
There is greens and cornbread
And dressing that's stuffed even chitterlings to
Burst your gut

Cakes and pies of every kind
Your pallet it anxiously waits
Turkey and mashed potatoes and
All of the trimmings are over running
The plates

Sweet potato pie and cranberry sauce
What dinner would be without it
Not putting my feet under someone's table
Be real I seriously doubt it

Ham, roast and potato salad
And those delicious steaming crescent rolls
Sitting at the table with bowed head and a grace
Then watch how the napkin unfolds

Some table awaits me be it morning or noon
It doesn't matter will sit with family will sit with friend
"I" like my pallet is anxiously waiting
for the rest of my body to join in.

Written By: Tressa Ann Olden

Curves

I walked into this place to get my body in shape
The coke bottle figure that I once had has somehow found an escape

I looked around the room at bodies' just like mine
Who had walked into this place you see in here we could refine

Step, step just keep on moving don't stop! Be the one who tries
Not only do you want that waistline but work push hard for those thighs

A month is gone; weight in time has come; you have worked hard and have given it your all
Step up on the scale with a positive outlook; mind set new clothes the mall!

A deep breathe as she measures each part; you smile she smiles 1 pound
Inches so many inches you've lost some weight
Heart lightened you set in for another round

Written by Tressa Ann Olden

God speaks through supernatural means

All scripture is breathed out by God and profitable for teaching, for reproof, for correction, and for training in righteousness.

2 Timothy 3:16

Freely

What happened when I gave my life to Jesus?
What happened when I let him freely in
What a peace in my mind and soul was miraculously released
Went were thoughts of worry thoughts of doubt thoughts of sin

God the father enters with his son Jesus
The Holy Spirit standing right there-by their side
When we lean not to our own understanding
We can ask him he will be there as our guide.

Holding on to our trembling bodies our trembling hands
Reassuring our doubting minds and broken hearts
Jesus Christ so ever faithful to his God given word
Having grace and mercy with all our life's struggles and life's starts

No matter how many times we come to him the Savior
He doesn't try or even keep a running account
Jesus tells us over and over again "bring it to me"
Cast your cares "I will surely work it out"

So everyday go beyond what seems unfamiliar
Don't be ashamed to cry out before God's heavenly throne
We all find rest in the master's strong embrace and loving arms
He knows each one of us and he's gracious not to leave us alone

Written by: Tressa Ann Olden

The power of God

Up on a cloud, down under the sea,
We see the handy works of God and
Marvel at what he has done,

Picturesque views, mountain top high we
are amazed at the rising of the sun.

Trees that know season of change,
Where the leaves fall swiftly, covering the ground

And down the slopes we see those with needles
Where the snow falls and never makes a sound.

The cool breeze from the wind, as it passes by;
A moon lit night at sunset in the evening hour

Wild flowers spreading across the field, a wet
dusty road after a morning shower.

Through this we see his works:
And God he alone spoke existence

Written by; Tressa A. Olden   2003

The Thought

I never feared losing you though death stood at the door.
God never let me near the thought that you would be no more.

The doctors said to one another we have done all that we can
Unknowingly they had given it over to Him, the true one in command

God took what would be grief and pain, and held it in His hand
And placed assurance deep in my heart I still don't understand.

All the days so quiet were they, many nights I thought of sorrows
But the God who knows our very thoughts assured me of many tomorrows

He gave me you, and you he gave me for He said," I not through with you yet."
We live each day knowing that he did for He's already paid the debt.

Those tears I shed were tears of gladness, His word is in my heart.
The vow still stands made long ago, until death do us part.

Written By: Tressa A. Olden   2004

Anchors

The stock anchors of any large ship often times go unnoticed and neglected
Used to hold the ship in place often times are set aside undetected

Most are made of iron and steel steadying the ship that makes it heavy weighting
I used the anchor to describe our mother's it's fitting that's all I'm saying

Wisdom being the rope, the chain the anchor cable that is steadfast to the ship
Resounding, unmovable and faithful to the Lord that faces life's storm with God's grip

Most ships carry two or more heavy anchors, God has blessed this family with all of these
Not often enough will you see them up speaking but rest assured they are bending their knees

Like anchors sometimes they need to be raised and lowered Solomon shared keep living and
your season will come
But don't mistake them for mere idlers they are aware of where their help comes from

Like steel they are very determined to keep running this Christian race
Like iron with its silver and white element they press toward the mark with a slow steady
pace.

They have lived what some only hope and dream of bye and bye with an understanding
everyday
Giving praises to the one and only Savior, who leads and guides their ageing footsteps all the
way.

Slow and steady they keep coming sending up timber, God's gifts they are not here by
mistake.
Precious souls left here to remind us of a loving Savior, a sovereign God and His favor Grace.

They are cornerstones, real diamonds in our churches they leave traditions and Legacy's from a gentler time
They are generations and generations of extended families here among us throughout the cities across God's Devine.

Seeing life changes so quickly everyday most live-in places where we can only hope to go
But if we don't take the time to ask them dear saints their history making, we will probably never know.

Each Sunday they sit right here in front of us, a smile, a wave, they give with splendor and glory.
We should often make a moment in this fast pace of life and take the time and listen to their story.

In this life promised only by God we would be pleased at some things they have done
How they came to live a life for the Savior and their belief in the true and living Son

Anchors, steadfast and steady sending timber up daily to the throne
Assembling themselves faithfully staying in the race until God calls them home

God Bless you

Tressa Ann Olden   2007

Beauty in the blackout

Confused, dismayed and desperate at times I was frightened and scared. I moved through life seemingly all by myself, I was hopeless and thinking no one cared. At times a light would guide me, but soon out the darkness appeared. I did not know which way to turn, my life was gone I feared. In darkness I could not find my way, thank God it was written on my heart. As I stumbled around from place to place the word recalled I would impart. Still trusting the word, I heard a sweet voice, though in darkness it guided me through. I have found through study God has no respect of persons; He will do the same for you. After a while I was guided out into a light, Hallelujah rang out of my mouth. My fears were calmed, my tears were all dry with an assurance everything was alright. When in life that I find myself with questions, I become still and with an ear I have learned. When you can't see your way that is dark or cloudy, His voice heard will guide all concerns. Now going on through life when I find myself, in dark places that I don't understand, I forge ahead moving to His beautiful voice who is standing without stretched hand. In the stillness I listen for the voice of Jesus, who is there with me and in command.....

Tressa   2009

Chance of a lifetime

Time comes and goes one knows not when
Your chance or time will come
It is measured only by fate I heard one say
But soon passes as a glimpse or a grin
Is it my time? Is it my time? You ask over again
With silence the only thing you hear
Is it my time? Is it my time? Repeating again
Hearing only so faint what is near
Time comes and goes so be ready
For no one knows exactly when
It is measure only by fate I heard one say
But soon passes as a glimpse or a grin

Written by:
Tressa Olden   2008

God still wants a yes!

I'm sad and broken hearted my mind is in a whirl
Each day confusion feels my heart consumptions causes a hurl
Yes, I am sick of this old world with all its vanity of things
I keep on asking the Savior for advice, to lead me with the trouble it brings
How can I do what is asked of me?
How do I get through the day? How can I live the life you have given me?
Which path is the right way?
Lord I'm disappointed with myself right now
Honestly, I don't even know which way to turn, my soul is crying out mightily to you
My thoughts my and ambitions I yearn.
What God I ask do you want from me? In this condition I can't even help myself
I'm lost and frustrated day after day, with all the self-help guides sitting on my shelf.
I asking you now, I can't reason this way, in this state where I need to get better
You are redemptive Lord, you're all-knowing Lord, you are powerful, you are greater!
What can I do to move from this place? What can I say to obey?
I said I'd go when you saved me Lord but certainly not this way

Disappointed, frustrated, down hearted, full of failures
God still wants a yes!

Written by: Tressa Olden   2008

God's Mercy

On a fast pace, no thoughts of destruction
Wondering this world, aimlessly without a care
Doing whatever I wanted, at anytime
Clueless or not concerned how it turned out or even fair

Year after year I woke up to another day
Seemingly thinking I did it all by myself
Putting behind me things that really mattered
Doing all in my power, leaving help knowledge on the shelf

Going on through life I found myself drawn
Into a world that offered "easy "as it's middle name
An intellectual gifted individual like myself
Excitement, fun, and success I could surely claim

And for a while I was on "Easy" street
It seemed my every thought fell into my lap
I got whatever I wanted when I wanted it
I had it all! Money, fame, and fortune dropped in the gap

And for years you couldn't say one thing to me
As a matter of fact, I was being asked for advice
Call my people was my response most of the time
And many turned to me and asked more than twice

Not sure what happened but one day I woke to nothing
My heart was heavy, my head was spinning and I felt sick
Still not sure how I came to this conclusion
Though I realized I had fallen into a trick

Big baller, shot caller is how they knew me
Expensive clothes, fancy cars all in a day
I was on my own and owing nothing to no one
Life to me was just a big game of play

All I could remember from that fallen day was my upbringing
Which right then seemed helpless to the cause for me
Where I was, needed intellectual attention
I was certain this was where I needed to be

Though being intellectual brought no help whatsoever
As a matter of fact, my thought patterns were not rational at all
Through learned upbringings I realized finally sin had put me here
And what I needed was to give "Mercy" a call

I had lost sight and put focus on this world and its material things
Remembering back, I now see where I went wrong
Living big, living large, was my main ticket
I had forgotten I am nothing on my own!

I cringed when I woke to the mornings
My self-centered-ness had allowed me to think I was boss
But thank you Jesus now greets my welcomed mornings
And hallelujah comes through, my praise of loss

First seek ye the kingdom of God is now my main thought
For sin had put me into this world's material trap
As I lay prostrate on the only thing, I had left
Calling for Mercy and allowing God now to stand in the gap

It wasn't easy, and for days, weeks, and months, I cried out for His mercy
Sin had taken away almost everything and pinned me down
All those people and those so call friends had disappeared on me
And my silk tie and jacket lay dampened somewhere on the ground

Continuing to pray I looked up again out of my window
And the sunshine had now for me a different glow
I stood up and walked out into the daylight
And stood there allowing the warmth I felt inside of me to flow

Today I have learned to give like there is no tomorrow
Of my time, my talent, and my tenth
I now know He wakes me every day refreshed, renewed
He holds tomorrow and remembers not where yesterday went

Thank God life for me now has a firm direction
Jesus anchors and guides my way and every footstep
My life that had become a mockery to myself and others
Through God's mercy and power, the restored me He kept

Tressa Olden   2008

God's provisions

Gods' provision's makes me:
Peacock Proud and Hyena Happy

It's no wonder when I get up in the morning
That I hum to myself a melody
A sweet, sweet song of assurance
That rest deep in the heart of me
I am seeing for the first time this morning
A new day one never seen before
I am realizing again God's goodness
Thanking him for He's the one I implore
Proud you say? Yes indeed! peacock proud!
Happy? Well hyena happy would describe it!
And the God I serve keeps providing for me
And abundance unmeasured to guide it!

Written by
Tressa Olden   2008

Hallow Days

Holidays are set aside for celebration, but hallow days are every day of the year

We hallow our Savior's name in our quiet time in referencing Him, He is ever so near

We hallow he is Jehovah Shalom He's peace that we need to survive

We hallow Jehovah Mckanesh His righteousness, He brings to our lives

We hallow he is Jevovah Tsidkunu, through separation He surely sanctifies

We know him daily as Jehovah Jarie, He's there and He always provides

At night when I lay on my pillow, Jehovah Shammad is always around

I hallow the name Jehovah Raphe, when my body or soul is bound

I call Jehovah Rohi my shepherd, He leads and directs my day

My banner is Jehovah Nissi, not hidden as I travel life's highway

All along my life's journey each day, my Savior's whatever I need Him to be

He is Jehovah Elohim the trinity our God is three

He can handle any situation; Almighty we know him as El Shaddai

He is greater than anyone or any power El Eljon our God most high

And so often we call upon Him, Lord God, Yhwh hallowing His name

He hears each one of His children's cries and loves us through our joy and our pain

Remembering we must hallow His name frequently, for He is worthy of each and every praise

Self-existent, Holy, and most wonderful our Father in all of His ways

When I stop and think of all that He is, praying daily with my voice His name I hallow

He is ever speaking to us with a small soft voice, I am Jesus the Great Jehovah, pray and follow

Written: Tressa Ann Olden   2005

I love you Lord

I love you Lord, I love you Lord, you hold me when I'm falling
I know you're there in every circumstance
And always you hear my calling
Your word is clear within my heart I repeat it over and over again
It takes me through some very rough times it soothes many nights of pain
Each day I thank you for loving me first and allowing me to love you too
I rest in YOU peacefully each awaking is so brand new

Tressa Olden   2008

I'm a lady

I always have a handkerchief
I'm a lady that's why!
I use it for so many things
Specially to wipe a tear from my eye
I can cover my legs when I'm sitting
Or with a wave I can say hello
My little hankie is very handy and it goes wherever I go!

Tressa Olden   2008

How, What, When Why

Often, I take a walk alone
Thinking and reminiscing my day
Panning over the events of life
Praying always along the way
How? comes across my mind sometimes
Can we live in this world full of sin?
Many times, we fail, we fall, we lose
Over and over again
What? I keep on asking
Are we supposed to do in this life?
To please the one who died for us
And not continue to live with strife
When? Will this road get easier?
Day to day it changes for not
As I look at this world's condition today
My savior assurance is all I've got
Why? Do I keep on walking? Why do I continue to forge ahead?
Why is daily answered for me
"I'll never leave you is what He said

Written by: Tressa Olden   2008

It's incredible

Looking out into this world
We have doubts about the things with no end
We try very hard to understand
And with our faces we place on a broad grin

Daily we travel from place to place
Seeking solutions to our many matters
Going all over finding answers to questions
And streamlining solutions that flatter us

I rather be out attending the sheep
Then busily moving around through the crowd
A peaceful place is what I seek
And volumes speak so very loud!

That to me is incredible
That I could think like this at this time
But I guess it only means there is a better place
And this thought has the worth of a dime!

Written by: Tressa Ann Olden

Only Jesus

Be careful as you go through life and don't just settle for anything!
Think through situations and talk them through to figure out what solutions each brings
Don't' live with regrets of should-a, could-a, would-a, when decisions are all up to you.
As you go through life consult the only guide who will be there to see you through….

Tressa Olden

Me

My life is but an open book, as page after page I turn
All the wrinkles and battle scars of years gone by
Are signs I have truly earned

A look in my mirror shows stories to be told
The failures, the successes all blend together
Aging memories bittersweet, and a dream of life getting better

There are memories of past things from birth till now
Growing up with trials and laughter
As each page is turned along the way, it connects from chapter to chapter

My life does unfold with each leaf happy or sad
Coming together to take its rightful place
My yoke is easy, my burdens light, most certainly gives me a steady pace

Today the leaves are still turning, and read out loud by many
Though hoping the life, I have lived is a beacon to all
And may the years left to me be plenty

Written by: Tressa Ann Olden   2008

Mr & Mrs (waiting room)

He looked at her face and smiled "I love you"
She returned his affection with a gentle blown kiss
I looked at the aged old couple and thought to myself, how long has it been and still have this

They acted as though they had just met
The love the sparkle I could see in their eyes
Plainly seen, was gray hair, wrinkles, glasses, and gold band
Though each had somehow now taken on a disguise

As I sat there watching them from across the waiting room
My imagination told a love story long before
She probably a gorgeous vixen and he a handsome gent
I sat thinking how much vested? How much in store?

Each one seemed removed from the body of wrinkles
In love were they in this world and free from cares
Only concerned were they for one another
Thinking now fondly of their many yester-years

I smiled when I heard him tell her she's beautiful
For her seen beauty had faded and long passed
She reached over and touched her handsome gentleman
Who she viewed stoutly, but comb over was on it's last?

Each saw one another I could plainly see now,
As though the years gone by had never been
Now knowing the affection shown in front of us all
Was their time spent together and love from within?

Written Tressa Ann Olden

162

Promise

He will supply your needs
Your daily bread and shelter you from the cold
He will clothe you when you are naked
And love you even after you're old
So live life to the fullest capacity, praying diligently everyday
Don't worry His eye is on the sparrow
He will guide you every step of the way

Written by: Tressa Olden   2008

She remembered

I walked into my grandma's room as she sat looking out on a view

A remembered gaze was on her face, of a time much gentler but true

I did not assuredly, want to disturb her, for her thoughts seemed to be occupied by a happier time

A soft sweet smile, was on her cheeks, of a bright and vibrant kind

I stood at her back very quietly

She didn't seem to know I was there

She just continued undaunted with her thoughts, that I hoped with me she'd share

After a while I walked very near her, and put my hand on her chair,

With a tremble in her voice, she said "how are you? I knew all the time you were there"

Oh, grand I did not want to disturb you. You seemed to be lost in thought anyway

"My child I am always reminiscing, when I'm waiting on my visit's each day"

Then she reached out her arms and embraced me, her body full of life though so fragile

Her hands I could see wore many wrinkles on them, but her mind was alert and very agile

Her touch felt so gentle and caring, as she held me close to her heart

A tear of joy ran down my face, our loved shared would never part

"So, my child I'm so glad to see you. You have come a mighty long way"

Oh, grand I would have traveled the globe for you. I know it is your birthday

"Dear child I'm just glad to see you. I've had so many I stopped counting long ago"

But grand we're so glad you're still with us, and we have all come to let you know

"Well, I'm glad to see each one of you. You all bring me so much joy"

"My children, grandchildren, and all the greats, every precious little girl and boy"

"And you granddaughter, do you remember, when I held you as a beautiful little child?"

Don't tell me grandmother you remember that? "I do" she said with a smile

"As a matter of fact, when they told me, it was you who'd be coming by, my mind went back to an earlier time" she said with a grandmother's sigh

So, grandmother is that what you were thinking about, when I came in and stood over there?

"Yes, child and if you're not in a hurry, take a sit and a story with you I will share"

Written by Tressa Olden   2009

Thoughts

When I thought life was hopeless, when I thought no one was there
When I wondered through life aimlessly in this world without a care
When I thought of being all by myself, when I thought I was all alone
When I thought of no one to talk to or even thoughts of going home
When thoughts of making it on my own, with my thoughts I abandoned fear
With thoughts I heard His soft sweet voice, with thoughts He drew me near
Thank God for Mercy

Tressa Olden   2008

Trusting

What is this anxiety within my soul I feel?
Uncertainty and loneliness lose footing won't heal
I sit and pray and wonder
A sure direction I need to find
What will I do to move from this place and find some peace of mind?
I trust the Savior is with me
He has never ever let me down
So often in this place I'm in He's consistently around
I need you Lord! Is my daily cry
I need your guiding hand
I need to know you have me here, Lord Jesus help me stand
I know my storm is temporary
When I put it in Your hand?
I must go on trusting in you, for you are my Savior in command
Anxious, unsure, lonely, throw in anger and bitterness too
I have trusted in you Lord a long time now
A break through is over due
And so dear Lord I am trusting, that you are listening to my heart
Whatever you have at the end of my storm will allow me a brand-new start

Love Tressa   2008

Yes? No?

Is it wise to say just to clarify be careful of your surroundings?
In this world of un-circumstance many happenings are very astounding
There was a time when no meant no, but now it just depends
The message that comes across today may be interrupted by whoever sends
Yes, was always a sure go ahead, though today it's very conditional
You did say yes? I did say yes only if
Oh stop! Oh my! what has happened to traditional?
Let's take a stand, let's not even waiver
We either do or we don't
Can't straddle the fence, can't have it both ways
Having it work, I'll tell you it won't
In looking at situations, there are always two sides
But remember with wisdom chose well
You cannot have your cake and eat it to
With careful watching you may still de-rail

Tressa Olden   2008

What?

He gave me you to angel
I'm still trying to understand why
We two are like day and night
What for you can I do?

I asked this question over and over
With answers that far surpass my thoughts
We are like oil and water
Yet He keeps sending me back to you

Tressa Olden   2009

The right man for the job

I admit I work better alone but prejudice I'm not. I work with all kinds and all colors.
Okay I'm a bit picky about what I work with. But given the right materials for the job,
I'm eye focused and yes, I use my head. Every job for me is given my undivided attention.
I will go in and out of a panel situation over and over again connecting every inch making
sure the customer is satisfied. I'm very sharp, straight forward and to the point. My name:
NEEDLE

Written by Tressa Olden   2009

ABC

When I was just a young child my mother taught me to pray. She said my child when you wake in the morning it will start you on your way. As a child I wanted so much to obey, but honestly, I was having some doubt. I sure didn't know just what to pray, to make anything work out. So, I went again to my mother, and shared with her my concern. She gave me a hug, and sat me down, and said this will help you learn. She sat down with me at the table, and wrote on paper and handed it to me. I looked at her and smile with a tease as I read A-B-C. I read each letter on the paper, as you know ended with Z. She instructed every morning while on your knees, repeat these letters you see. So, every single morning before I left for my day, I GOT OUT MY PIECE OF PAPER AND I BEGAN TO SAY: A-B-C-right down to the end, not sure but it made me feel better. How something so simple could be called a prayer, just by re-sighting a single letter. Now much older in life I went to my mother and asked about her method. She said my child God understands and meets you until you get it. When you were five, I knew you had learned, every letter of your A-B-C-'S. It's important to know when we pray to God, pray doubtless and open and free. When we pray to God it's the fervent heart, that he hears and understands. It's not the words we say, he interprets our cry, and yes, he is in command. Now all grown you, I still remember, every morning my A, B, C,'s. The letters all have added elements but each is so real to me. A is for his assurance, B is for his bloodshed, C is for Christ His son, and on and on just as she said.

Tressa Olden   2009

Years

It had been two years when the encounter occurred. Neither had frequented the same places or visited the neighborhood park where they met. Unfortunately, both found themselves on the same aisle at the grocery store. With the holiday crowd neither were able to U-turn without being noticed by the other, both forged reluctantly ahead. Slowly they moved toward one another. She held tight to her cart that boasted a bottle of Merlo and two large T-bones. He on the other hand was hoping his cart that was carrying a single red rose would grow wings and fly away. Their eyes met. It was awkward. "How are you? He asked. She wanted to say "fine" but she wasn't and nothing came out. What each felt was going to take longer than a grocery visit. Both forced a smile and moved on. Time had stood still. Love hurts!

Tressa Olden   2009

172

Crossroads

Here I am at a crossroad, and wondering where to turn
My thoughts are going in all directions, my outcome is of concern
I know I want to take that step; I know I want to leap
I know I can taste success someday, my failures they just heap
But I can't give in to failure, for nothing beats it but a try
I have to stop procrastinating, and accept my wings and fly...
This is my year, this is my time, it is closer than you think
I am prepared to try again, if failures cause me to sink...
Though I will never know the road, until I make that move
Will I sink, or will I fly, landing safely in my groove
This is my year, this is my time, it is closer than you think
What I have been striving for all this time, is right there on the brink!

Tressa Ann Olden   2011

My Savior

Sometimes I'm not quite sure of my standing ground
I rely and lean on my Saviors embrace
So often unsure of what He has in store
Are even what in life I must face?

Restless nights, long days, without any answers
Uncertainty, disappointment is in range
I keep praying to the only one that's listening
For through Him I know this situation can and will change

I am struggling trying to do just what my bible says
You know! To love those who despitefully use you
So daily I go to my Savior with my feelings
With His mercy and His grace, He restores me new

So, when in times of disappointments
And the road ahead I cannot even see
I know my loving Savior is there with me
To instruct and guide, where and what I am to be

So often I go to Him so very heavy hearted
And this world we live in goes on seemly without fear
I am glad that I know a wonderful risen Savior
His word I've hidden in my heart to keep Him near

Written by: Tressa Olden

An angel among us

Very little to nothing was voiced, but her presence spoke loud to many.

Voices by many a passerby surrounded her starring from a distant. A friendly touch, a hug affectionately aimed from a few. What did she feel? How did she share what was in her, that screamed out silently? Most cared for her, many loved her, though few understood her. And those who did received

Tressa Olden   2009

New Day

I woke up to the morning, a new day never seen before. My mind and open window, with a blank canvas I head through the door. What will this new day bring for me? Who will I see or greet? What new challenges will be ushered in? What life changing encounter will I meet. I look UP realizing a new day granted with all the endless possibilities!

Tressa Ann   2009

Every Woman

I was rejected like a bondwoman named Hagar and honored like a woman named Sarah; my extreme needs were always met by the Lord; life goes on and daily I say dare I?

Often like Lot's wife, I didn't take God's grace seriously, like Leah an unhappy marriage I did boast: my extreme needs were always met by the Lord: life goes on and daily I made of it the most.

Like Jochebed I considered sorrow my friend, like Tamar I needed to vindicate my right; my extreme needs were always met by the Lord; life goes on and daily I fight a good fight.

Like Deborah I was inspired by faith, like Naomi I certainly cared about others; my extreme needs were always met by the Lord; life goes on and daily I remember to love my brothers.

Often like Orpah I made bad decisions, and like Ruth I was ever so loyal: my extreme needs were always met by the Lord; life goes on and daily moving, not stagnant to spoil.

Like Abigail I watched over God's servant. And as sweet Huldah I help lead a nation back to God; my extreme needs were always met by the Lord; life goes on and daily praying, feet shod.

And like Mary Magdalene I led the way following Christ, and Mary of Jerusalem my house functioned for God; my extreme needs were always met by the Lord; life goes on and daily as Moses in our hand there is a rod.

Yes, there are so many other's I could name, and at any time we could resemble any one, our extreme needs are always met by the Lord; life goes on and daily we need His precious SON!

Written by: Tressa Olden   2008

Don't

Don't be-little yourself to other's
Don't put yourself down that way
Don't agree or participate when others are cruel
Don't acknowledge what they continue to say

Do lift and hold your head up high
Do smile and bring a brighter tomorrow
Do love yourself in a positive way
Do it now and free yourself of worried sorrow

Written by: Tressa Olden

Fruit of the season

I love fresh peaches in the summer
The sweetness of its juice running down my face
A napkin! A napkin! I would yell for assistance
To save myself from a bit of disgrace.

Careful, be careful, I keep telling myself
With this large delicious fruit in my hand
Every bite is utterly inviting
This round fuzzed morsel of which I command

Bite after bite is so yummy
Putting it down is not even my thought
My teeth going inside as I hold it out from me
Being careful using the manners I was taught

Whoa! You're really enjoying yourself
I could hear from someone at the table
Yes, I smiled saying as I continued to eat
Offering it up as I removed the fruit's label

Yum, yum, yum! That was good I said finishing
Every bite was worth the juices I did drop
It's good and healthy and nourishing too
Clean up time now I'm finished I'll stop

Written by: Tressa Ann Olden

God Speaks

Through our consequences

The heart is deceitful above all things, and desperately wicked: who can know it?

I the Lord search the heart, try the reins, even to give every man according to his ways, and according to the fruit of his doings.

Jeremiah 17:9-10

The Starving Time

It's a hard time in Jamestown in 1809. The winter is coming and as the old folks say, it's starving time. We are trying to grow some crops like carrots, mushrooms, pumpkins, and corn, but the weather is not in our luck. My plan is to make a home for the crops but there's a problem, I don't have enough money.

I was going around the town as the wind was blowing against my body, like I was in the Antarctic. I walked up to an old man and asked if he needed any help, and he said, "well in fact I do." I need to make a house before the winter hits, I explained. You never know you may learn some building skills. The old man and Adam worked all day and night. After they were done Adam was able to get 20 pounds. He was so grateful he also learned some tips on building. He was so happy and delighted.

Its time, winter is here. If you go outside the wind will stalk you like an eagle in the sky. The town is slowly dying. Our crops are getting low even with them being protected. It's colder than polar bears home here. I know for a fact that a lot of people will not make it. And since there is no sunlight it's hard to grow the crops. But living is the hardest part.

Isaiah Olden

Beyond the egg

Beyond the egg is the cross, where Jesus died for me
Beyond the egg is the reason, that I've been called and yes, I'm free
Beyond the egg our Savior, gave victory to the grave
Beyond the egg there is assurance, that in Jesus Christ I am saved
So, let's not get caught up in bunnies, color eggs and baby chicks
Beyond the egg is so much more that our Savior came to fix
With His sacrifice we were bought, a price we could not pay
So, we should go to him thank fully, each and every day
And as we approach Easter morning, the egg and all of its attention
Go to your bible a read for yourself these chapters and verses I've mentioned

Matthew 27:32-56 Mark 15:21-38 Luke 23:26-49 John 19: 16-37

Written by: Tressa Olden   2021

Open bible

There was much I was searching for
I opened my bible to find the truth
I heard the stories passed down through the years
For myself now, I read the proof

Jesus paid a price that I could not
One day on Calvary
Whipped, bruised and beaten He took it all
So that I would be made free

All night they tried my savior
Torturing of Him, I thought would never end
Though He hung right there until He gave up the ghost
Paying a debt for all of my sin

Jesus paid the ultimate price
That day on the old rugged cross
For our God knew without His son
All of this sinful world would be loss

I'm so thankful for His sacrifice
His forgiveness of my sin truly is
He welcomed me with opened arms
Praise God He called me His

Written by: Tressa A. Olden   2021

The End

www.ingramcontent.com/pod-product-compliance
Lightning Source LLC
Chambersburg PA
CBHW041114120626
46547CB00019B/2711